Recollections

Andrew Jackson Chambers

Ye Galleon Press

Fairfield, Washington

1975

For individuals who may wish to have more information on this pioneer family the Washington State Historical Society, Tacoma, has published a booklet, The Thomas M. Chambers Collection, a Bibliographical Guide.

Library of Congress Cataloging in Publication Data

Chambers, Andrew Jackson, 1825-1908.
    Recollections.

    "Reminiscences (by) Margaret White Chambers": p.
    1. Overland journeys to the Pacific. 2. Chambers, Andrew Jackson, 1825-1908. 3. Chambers, Margaret White.
I. Chambers, Margaret White. Reminiscences. 1975. II. Title.
F593.C47   1975   978'.02'0924 (B)   75-45379
ISBN 0-87770-156-3

Recollections

The Andrew Jackson Chambers booklet was printed in 1947, 102 years after his journey was made. Only a few copies were made and these are now difficult to obtain, with copies quoted up to eighty-five dollars in antiquarian book dealer catalogs. The Margaret White Chambers turn of the century booklet is appended.

Three hundred-fifty copies were printed in the workshop of Glen Adams in the winter of 1975-1976.

This is Copy Number 279 .

RECOLLECTIONS

Crossing the Plains in 1845

My father's reading Lewis and Clark's Journal was the cause of our crossing the plains. We started the 1st of April, 1845. Our company consisted of my father, Thomas M. Chambers, mother, Letitia Chambers, five brothers, James W., David J., Thomas J., Andrew J. (myself), John, and McClain, and two sisters, Mary Jane and Letitia. My brothers, James and David, were married and their wives, Mary and Elizabeth, accompanied them.

We started from Morgan County, Missouri, and crossed the Missouri River on a ferry at St. Joe. This place marked the last of the settlements. From this point we traveled the old emigrant road up the Platte River. Our journey led us through portions of what are now the states of Missouri, Kansas, Nebraska, Wyoming, Idaho, Oregon, and Washington. Then this was a wilderness with only the old tracks of emigrants that had passed that way in 1834-35. We crossed the Kaw River, about forty miles from St. Joe, on a ferry, after that we forded all the streams to which we came. The first day that we saw buffalo, on the South Platte River, it was buffalo as far as the eye could see. We camped and killed fifteen that evening. It took two days to jerk all the meat we wanted. Buffalo and antelope were plentiful for twelve or fifteen hundred miles. Hunters sometimes put a handkerchief up on a stick and the antelope came around to see what it was, and often we killed them by shooting from the wagons. We had to go out to the edge of the hills to hunt buffalo, except the first day we saw them, of which I have just spoken.

ANDREW JACKSON CHAMBERS

Opposite Ash Hollow we crossed the Platte River, which, though wide and shallow was difficult to ford on account of quicksand. We passed near Chimney Rock, which rose like a great chimney from the level country. We could see this landmark for a number of days and passed it within five or six miles.

At Fort Laramie on the North Platte River, measles broke out in our family and we had to lay by fifteen days. We had overtaken other westward bound wagons on our journey and our party was now thirty wagons. While being detained here, about one thousand wagons passed us, and most of our company joined a party and left us at Laramie.

From Fort Laramie we traveled to Fort Hall in Idaho. We had tried traveling with large and with small companies. We found that we got on much faster in small companies but it was very hard to stand guard with only a few in the party. We fell in with a company of fifty wagons. Their teams had been scared by the Indians and had gotten into the habit of stampeding. They stampeded one day while we were with them. It was terrible to see fifty teams running, each team of three or four yoke of cattle— about three yoke of cattle was an average team. There was no way of holding them back except to hang on to the yokes and call to the cattle. It was an anxious time for the women and children in the wagons. One ox fell and broke his neck. This was the last day we traveled with them. After Fort Laramie we had fallen in behind these wagons with what remained of our old company. This is all that saved us from the stampede on that day.

This event recalls the first Indians we saw. Father was captain of the company. He ordered the wagons into two lines, the women and children to stay in the wagons, except those that could carry guns. I can recollect seeing mother marching along carrying a rifle. All the horses and cattle were driven into the enclosure made by the wagons to protect them from stampeding. We never stopped but marched along with the wagons in two lines and the horses and cattle between them.

Father stepped out to meet the chief who was coming toward us. The Indians seemed friendly but wanted tobacco. As soon as father gave one tobacco, another would step up and say, "Me, big chief, too." Father gave them all that he had in his pouch. There was a large camp of the Indians, and it appared that this was a war party and that they had been out to fight other Indians. They were now on their way home.

On much of our way wood was very scarce. We always sent a party ahead of us to find wood, grass, and water. We found buffalo chips plentiful for at least a thousand miles, and often we had to use them altogether for fuel. On the Sweet Water, in Wyoming, we caught a great many nice fish.

From Fort Hall we traveled to Fort Bridgers, which was two hundred miles north of Salt Lake. It was really no fort at all. A man by the name of Bridgers was located here and carried on trade with the Indians and with the emigrants. From here we went to Salmon Falls, on the Snake River, and here we met a few Indians, but they were friendly. Until we crossed the Rockies, through the Devil's Gate, we traveled up hill and up stream, but after we crossed the Snake River the waters flowed westward and we could almost see where the divide came.

ANDREW JACKSON CHAMBERS

From Salmon Falls we traveled two or three days down the river before we crossed. We found a place where there was an island in the river. We crossed to the island first, and then went diagonally across the rest of the river which was about three-fourths of a mile wide. We always took horses and rode across the rivers we had to ford and found out exactly where the wagons ought to go. The fords were always thoroughly prospected before the teams were driven into the water. We found at this crossing the deepest part was eight or ten feet wide, and deep enough to swim the cattle, the rest of it averaged about two feet. We blocked up the wagon beds as high as the standards would allow, to keep our goods dry, and hitched on ten or twelve yoke of cattle to the first wagon. The other wagons were fastened together one behind the other. There was a chain attached to the tongue of the wagon following and that in turn to the hind axletree of the forward wagon. The drivers went to the lower wide of their teams to keep the cattle braced up against the current and to keep the direction slanting up stream. They had to hold on to the bows of the yokes to keep themselves braced up, too. By the time all the teams were in the water, the lead teams were in shallow water, and we were finally safely over without wetting any of our goods. Shortly after this our oxen began to give out. We became uneasy for fear we could not travel across the mountains which were before us, on account of snow. To be caught on the east side of the mountains meant almost certain death. We began to break in the cows. We started across the plains with about twenty milch cows. By the time we reached The Dalles, in Oregon, we had almost all the cows broken in. They were lighter on their feet and traveled much better than the oxen. We didn't know at that time that we would have saved our cattle's feet by providing ourselves with shoes and nails before leaving the states.

Three or four days before we came to Fort Boise we were camped on a creek, and when supper was ready and each one had sat down to his place at the table on the ground, an Indian standing there knelt down at the place intended for a man named Smith. As soon as Smith finished washing himself he knocked the Indian over with a stick and took the place himself. Sticks which the Indians had used for digging roots or for some other purpose were lying around plentifully. The Indians looked very sullen after this and next morning one of the horses was gone, stolen. We traveled on as though nothing had happened for two days and came to a place where we thought it advisable to rest the cattle a day, there being good grass and water there. James Chambers, Smith and myself concluded that evening to ride back to the place where we had lost the horse, and it might be, we could find an Indian camp and do something terrible. Smith wanted to kill an Indian. We rode all night and when we reached the place another party of emigrants was camping there, and we found an Indian at the camp on the stolen animal. Smith had felt all the time that his act had been the cause of our losing the horse, and he was very anxious to straighten things out by killing an Indian. Brother James went around the camp one way and I another. I came upon the Indian and horse and I caught the horse. Immediately Smith insisted on shooting the Indian but some of the campers interfered. They contended that we were out of the way, and that if we killed an Indian his friends would come and take revenge on them. They also argued that maybe this was not the Indian that stole the horse, and they urged us to make the women in camp feel easy by releasing the Indian. After consulting for some time, we agreed to let the Indian go, and to give him something for scaring him nearly to death. He was so badly frightened great drops of sweat came out on his face. The next thing we had to consider was what to give the Indian. As it was coming on the fall of the year, Mother had supplied us well with shirts. I had enough to last me two years, and I had on two at this time. They agreed that I must pull off one of my shirts and give it to the Indian. So I did, and all parties concerned, except myself, were well pleased, the Indian most of all.

From Boise we traveled to Grand Ronde, and after we passed the valley and came down off the Blue Mountains into the Umatilla Valley, we saw lots of Indians. Mary Jane, my sister, was then a comely girl about sixteen years of age. Indian chiefs offered Father fifty horses and a hundred blankets for her. They didn't care whether the girl was willing, they wanted a white klootchman. This scared Mary Jane, and she didn't want to show herself when the Indians were around.

When we were within a few day's journey of The Dalles, and after we had crossed the DesChutes River, two horses were stolen from us. We went back from Fifteen Mile creek to a village near by and called on the chief. He said he would have the Indians bring in the horses. They claimed that the horses had been stolen by some bad Indians and that a good Indian brought them back, and that he ought to have pay for it. We had become accustomed to paying, so we were prepared to give a shirt. This satisfied them.

RECOLLECTIONS

Our trip had not been a pleasure trip, for from the time we left St. Joe each one of us had to stand guard about once a week, and from the time we left Fort Boise each one had to stand guard half the night every other night, and after having the measles this was no fun.

On October 15th we arrived at The Dalles. On account of the lateness of the season we selected a place for winter quarters. This was on a creek about two miles from the Methodist mission.

Here, in November, we built huts for the family and large corrals of logs in which to keep the horses for safety, at night. We watched them during the day. Our cattle were at large. We looked after them to prevent their straying too far. We drove them together a few times every day. Several parties left their stock in our care during the winter.

As soon as the family was in its winter quarters, Father and I went down the Columbia River and up the Willamette River for a winter's supply of flour. This was about the 20th. of November. At Oregon City we bought a skiff and one thousand pounds of flour. A young man by the name of Scoggins and myself started out to take the flour to the family.

Father stayed down the Willamette in Tualatin plains all winter, looking for places in which to locate. When we reached The Dalles, James and his wife left their stock with us, their oxen had given out, and went on, and Father remained with James and his wife until spring.

Scoggins and I started with plenty of provisions for our trip, which we calculated would be seven days. On account of stormy weather we were seventeen days. Below Cape Horn, on the

Columbia, we had to lay by in one place two days. Cape Horn is a rocky spur of the Cascade Range, two or three hundred feet high and almost perpendicular.

This was the hardest seventeen days work I ever did. It appeared to storm almost all the time. We had the flour in sacks of one hundred pounds each, and we loaded and unloaded them sometimes eight or ten times a day. The wind would stop blowing for a time, and by the time we got loaded and ready to start, it would begin again, and we would be obliged to unload, for the river was so rough. The wind blew either up steam or down stream. The family needed the flour badly and we were anxious to get to them with it. Some days we would not go over a mile, after working hard all day, and then the wind would apparently abate when we could not avail ourselves of the calm. Our supply of provisions were soon about all used up except the flour. Flour and water without even salt was not very good to keep up either spirits or strength. We mixed the water and flour together in the top of the sack and made the dough into long strings which we wrapped about a stick. We set the stick by the fire and baked the dough, which tasted pretty good, after a hard day's work. We varied this with noodle soup made of water and flour. We were three days making the five miles of rapids and seven hundred yards of portage The last day on the rapids our boat took a sheer and the one on shore had to pull so hard against the current that the boat filled with water. In the face of this calamity I thought the family would starve. I was twenty years of age, but in my anxiety I cried. This was the first, last, and only time I cried while crossing the plains.

RECOLLECTIONS

We finally got the boat to a safe place and bailed it out. We were sure our flour was ruined. We took the sacks out and let the water drain off, reloaded and proceeded on our journey.

That night we built a fire and dried the sacks and found the flour was not hurt much. We were lucky to find two white men and three Indians to help us carry our boat over the portage. Four days of travel up the river brought us to our winter home. We found all well and anxious for our return .

ANDREW JACKSON CHAMBERS

*First Flat-Bottomed Boat to Cross Over
the Cascade Falls. 1846-1847*

As I have said, Father remained down the Willamette the winter of 1845 with brother James and wife, looking for a place, and the middle of January, 1846, he and James came back to The Dalles to help build a boat to move us.

There were plenty of boats then on the Willamette for emigrants who wanted to pass on down to the valley, but a very short time after we arrived at The Dalles they were all taken off.

James was a boat builder. We selected a place close to the river to build our boat where there was good timber. We chose two large trees for the purpose of making gunnels for each side of the boat, the trees being about three feet in diameter. Then we picked out smaller trees for making the plank. We hewed out the timber the proper length and squared it. This we lined on both sides the thickness we wanted to make our planks. We chose a place on a side hill to make a saw-pit. It was so arranged that one man could stand underneath the log and one man on top of it. Then the squared logs were put in place and we ripped out enough plank for a bottom and false bottom, and for the sides of the boat. We used the old whip-saw now on exhibition in the Oregon Historical Rooms in Portland. This whip-saw told its own story in an Olympia paper in 1894 as follows:

"I started for Puget Sound from Missouri in 1845, and after passing through the trials and incidents of an overland journey of six months, reached The Dalles, Oregon, where, with the assistance of four men, I sawed timber enough to construct a boat sixteen feet wide and fifty feet long. On February 1, 1846, the boat was loaded with myself among the passengers, and we moved down the Columbia to the Cascades. At the Cascades I took passage in a wagon around a five-mile portage. Our boat was the first boat sent over Cascade Falls. The craft was secured, and proceeded to the mouth of Sandy River. From that point my travels varied, sometimes by land and sometimes by water, up one stream and down another. Finally, in the spring of 1848, I reached Puget Sound, after a tedious journey behind an ox team. In the three years of my travels, my master always found me of service, and during the past forty-seven years, I resided undisturbed and unthought of in my master's tool house, on Chambers Prairie. On April 26, 1894, the flames destroyed my home and I was ruined and defaced almost beyond recognition."

The story of the whip-saw being told, to resume, —We had no nails and the boat was put together entirely with wooden pins. It resembled a scow of today. Its capacity was large enough to carry fifteen head of cattle at a time in crossing the river, and to store away all our wagons, taken apart, and all our plunder that we had brought with us across the plains, also those members of the family who were ot on shore driving the cattle.

When we got the boat ready and launched, we loaded our effects, wagons, plunder, and ox yokes, and proceeded down the Columbia River.

When we collected our stock, to make the start, our cattle were in good condition. The snow rarely stayed on the southern slopes of the hills and the cattle had opportunity to do well. But not so with the horses. The Indians had managed to steal most of them during foggy weather, when it was pretty hard work to guard tnem. We did not have more than three horses out of the lot whose manes and tails had not been cut off. The mutilated animals looked horrible to us. There was always some good Indian to help us hunt the stolen animals. It appeared the Indians did not want the horses except to have a big ride on them, and to get their manes and tails. they made ropes out of the hair.

Our boat had long oars, and when we started two men attended to these. Brother James usually steered the boat, and Father and David were aboard most of the time. We let the boat run with the current as great a distance each day as we could drive the cattle. Then we tied up and resumed our course next morning. We traveled on the south side down the river bottom until we came to Shell Rock, a place where the hills came right up to the river's edge. We could not drive over the rock, neither could we swim the cattle around it. Here we ferried all our effects and cattle to the north side and traveled down the north shore until we came to the Cascade Falls. At this point we unloaded our wagons, put them together, loaded our plunder into them, hitched up the teams, and started out to make our way to the lower end of the falls.

Everything had been removed from the boat, and the sides boarded up. Brother James, and two men who were willing to take the risk, went aboard. He acted as captain and they stood at the oars. We had several small boats, so we took her out in the river and gave her a good start, heading her straight for the falls. She went over, shipping only a nominal number of gallons of water. It was in February that we made this run with the first flat-bottomed boat ever to pass over these five miles of rocks and rapids.

RECOLLECTIONS

Having gotten safely over, they tied up and returned to help us with teams and stock. We had to blaze a trail to go through and prospect a road. We were obliged to go back about a mile from the river and pass through an Indian graveyard. In this graveyard the dead were all buried in houses, and we had to drive carefully between them. It was an ancient burying place, for the houses were all decaying. I think it would not have been used for many, many years.

After traveling about six miles we came again to the river just below the lower falls. We reloaded the boat and proceeded as before. The drivers took the cattle along by the river until they reached Cape Horn. Here we were obliged again to leave the river and travel out into the country and around this high promontory. We had to drive very slowly and it was hard work. On this trip we took a little flour, salt, and enough bread to do us the first day out. After that we tied up the calves so that we could get milk enough to make noodle soup with milk, flour, and salt. It was nearly three days before we reached the river again. At the mouth of Sandy River we found the scow and the folks waiting for us. Here we unloaded again and ferried our stock across to the southern side of the Columbia at the mouth of the Sandy. From this point we drove the cattle across the country by Oregon City to Milk Creek, close to Molalla, where Father had selected a place for us.

After ferrying the stock across at the mouth of the Sandy, we unloaded the boat with our effects, and ran down the Columbia to the Willamette and up the latter river to Oregon City. Here we sold the boat for fifty dollars. We put our plunder in the wagons and moved out to the place selected for our future home, and set to work to build houses in which to live.

ANDREW JACKSON CHAMBERS

The citizens of Oregon were of the opinion that Uncle Sam was slow in extending protection to his people on the Pacific slope, and they formed a provisional government and elected Abernathy governor. The representatives passed laws, saying that a married man and his wife could take up six hundred and forty acres—a milesquare—of land; a young, or single man, half that amount, and this could be selected any place so that it did not interfere with other claims. Wheat was made legal tender for small debts at one dollar a bushel.

Oregon City being located at the falls on the Willamette River, the Hudson's Bay Company had a flour mill and a store there. Up the Willamette, the old servants of the company had settled and taken up a great many of the choice places for fifty or sixty miles. One prairie called "French Prairie," was settled by the Canadian French, and most of these settlers had native wives.

The first settler here, cut hazel brush and made withes with which to bind their wheat. At this time the sickle and reaphook were used. Then the cradle came into use and the people learned to make bands of the wheat, and other grain that was cut.

After putting in one spring crop and garden in Molalla, we built a barn. I then went to Tualatin Plains, west of Oregon City, and stopped with brother James and family. He married a Mrs. Scoggins, who had a family of five children, three sons and two daughters. I, together with these children, went to school one term. The oldest son was one of my best friends, and it was he who helped me take the flour up the Columbia to my folks.

RECOLLECTIONS

Tualatin Plains, twenty miles from Oregon City, was settled principally by Hudson's Bay men, English and Scotch. This was a fine section of the country. Plenty of wheat was grown here, and newcomers could get plenty of work by taking pay in wheat at one dollar a bushel. The wheat could be taken to Oregon City, and sold to the company and taken out in trade in the store, and a receipt for the remainder would be given. This receipt could be used for anything wanted, and they, in turn, could go to the store and get goods and groceries with it. There was very little money in the country, so people were obliged to use wheat and these receipts, as a means of conducting business transactions. The emigrants to this country had spent, mostly, all their money for outfits and a great many, even then, were very poorly provided with provisions for the trip.

After school closed I stayed with my brother James and helped in the harvest. The barns were built of logs, two houses and a space of thirty feet between them, the roof including the three. The center was used for a threshing floor, and ten or twelve horses were used to tramp out the wheat. The farmers would furnish us with horses and board, and give us one bushel in ten, to thresh out and fan the wheat, and sometimes they allowed us a team to take the wheat to market. While I was helping my brother that harvest, I did the threshing and my brother and young Scoggins hauled in the sheaves. We threshed eighty to ninety bushels a day.

One of the oldest settlers came to my brother and wanted help. James told him that I could go, and wanted to know how much he would pay me per day. The old settler said he would give me three pecks of wheat a day. James told him I might remain home and play before I should work for that price. I told my brother to make a contract with him to cut and shock his wheat, and young Scoggins and I would do the work as soon as we finished his (my brother's) crop. He made the contract at three bushels an acre and board.

We put in thirty acres for him. We put up three acres a day, and the old gentleman was highly pleased with our work. His wheat was getting very ripe and shattered out, so that he proposed for us to cut and bind in the forenoon and haul in the afternoon, and he would pay us just the same per day for the hauling; that was nine bushels a day.

It was hard for him to keep help. One harvest was all that help would stay with him. Some of his help told that he recommended them to eat the peelings off baked potatoes. He said it was healthy and helped to fill up. I think he was correct about it being good for the health if he followed his own advice, for he lived to be one hundred and four years old.

The winter of 1846 we spent in looking for a new location, thinking to better ourselves. We went to the mouth of the Columbia River and looked over Clatsop Plains, then south to the Umpqua country, but we did not find anything to suit us.

Father said he had started out for salt water, so, in the spring of 1847, we again put in the crops, and then came over to Puget Sound to look at that portion of the country. We spent two months looking around. At Newmarket, the present site of Tumwater, at the falls of the Deschutes River, we found M. T. Simmons and family, and five or six other families and nine or ten young men. They had settled here in June, 1845. They were putting up a saw mill. They already had a flour mill, a very small concern. The burrs were only eighteen inches in diameter and no bolting cloth was in use. Some of the families had sieves that were used to take out the coarse bran.

At the present site of Olympia there was one man by the name of Smith. His log cabin stood on the ground where the Huggins hotel is now. We finally staked out claims on what is now known as "Chambers Prairie." We then returned to our homes in Oregon to make preparations to move to the Puget Sound region in the fall.

ANDREW JACKSON CHAMBERS

Settlement on Puget Sound

Early in the fall of 1847, we hired two boats from Dr. McLoughlin, and four Kanaka boatmen. We loaded our effects, wagons, ox-yokes, and bedding on the boats at Oregon City. We went down the Columbia to the mouth of the Cowlitz, and up the Cowlitz to Cowlitz Landing—thirty miles.

It was fine boating until we came to the rapids on the Cowlitz River. There it was hard work and slow traveling. We had to use the tow line a great deal and go from one side of the river to the other to take advantage of the eddies and shallow water, so that we could use the long poles to push the boat upstream. Our boats were heavily laden and for about fifteen miles, we used the poles and tow line, the water being too swift for oars.

There was a great quantity of salmon in the river. We had all that we wanted and cooked it Indian fashion. This was, to dress the fish, run a stick through it and place the stick in the ground close to the fire, and, as the fish cooked, turn it so that it would bake evenly. We always left the scales on until it was cooked. After working hard all day, it was fine!—we thought delicious.

We arrived at Cowlitz Landing after twenty days of travel, the only accident on the trip being the loss of a rifle, a considerable loss in those days, too.

In making this trip to Cowltiz Landing, we started the hands with the stock, horses and cattle, to cross the Columbia. All were ferried over at Fort Vancouver, then they were driven up the Cowlitz and swam the South Fork. When they reached Cowlitz Landing, they swam the stock to the north side of the river and waited for the boats. This landing is a the lower end of Cowlitz Prairie. This prairie was settled by the Canadian French and it is a fine farming country. The Hudson's Bay Company and the Catholic Mission each had fine farms there. We rented twenty acres of land from the Catholic Mission and twenty acres from John R. Jackson and put in a crop of winter wheat.

When the crop was in we left the stock needed to haul our wagons to the prairie (Chambers) which we had selected for our future home, and started to drive the remainder of the stock through. We drove them over Mud Mountain, or Mud Hill—all the first settlers traveled this way, and we crossed the Deschutes about two miles above Tumwater. There was an Indian trail from Bush Prairie to Chambers Prairie.

Then we went back to Sanders' Bottom and completed the wagon road around Mud Mountain. This hill is east of Chehalis. There was one family living there at that time. We prospected and blazed out a road. We found trees on the bank of the creek that suited us for making a bridge. We built the bridge and cut out a wagon road through Sanders' Bottom, a distance of three miles. The creek's source was from Mud Mountain and the banks were steep and muddy and could not be crossed without a bridge. We then came to New Market, one of the very first settlements at Tumwater. The men of this settlement turned out and all helped to cut out a wagon road to Chambers Prairie, a distance of three and a half miles. The old settlers here were glad to see newcomers and they were ready and willing to help us. What they had they were willing to share with us. They were much pleased when they learned that we had sieve wire, so that they could take the coarse bran out of their flour. On the prairie we built a log house of two rooms; the smaller one we used for a kitchen and the larger one was curtained off into bed rooms. We then went for the family and brought them over. We stopped a few days with Mr. Simmons' family.

We crossed our wagons on boats when the tide was in, below the lower falls of the Deschutes, near where the old Biles house stands. When the tide was out we drove our work cattle across Budd's inlet, and then drove out five miles to our future home. The fifteenth day of December, 1847, we took our first dinner at our home on Chambers Prairie.

Here, our stock had plenty of grass and wintered well, and they were fat in February. We butchered a fine beef and had plenty of tallow to make candles, and we were glad to have candles. Mother brought enough candle wicking to do several years. The candles were a great improvement on the old iron lamp in which we had to burn hogs' lard. This lamp was made with a short spout for the wick to lie in, and one end of the wick came out in this spout to burn. The handle at the other end of the lamp was so arranged that it came up over the center of the lamp, so as to hold the lamp level. With a small chain this lamp could be hung up. A cotton cloth, twisted, served as a wick.

Father put up a milk house and in March commenced to make butter, and in April, to make cheese.

Brother Thomas and I took up claims adjoining, and we milked the cows morning and evening for our board. We built a log house of one room on our claim. We made it a five cornered house, the fifth corner being for the fireplace. In May we dug two troughs and started a tan yard, on a small scale. We used the troughs for vats, and alder and hemlock bark for tanning purposes. We dried the bark and pounded it fine. We burned oyster and clam shells and used the lime to take the hair off the skins. We made sole leather out of beef hides, and for the upper leather, we used deer and cougar hides.

By the first of November, we had our leather ready to make shoes. We brought a kit of shoe-makers' tools with us, and father and I made the shoes. I made the ladies' shoes. We brought with us a number of lasts of different sizes.

For sewing thread we put a number of strands of shoe thread together—the length we wanted—and we twisted and waxed this string, tapered the ends, and put a hog bristle on each end for needles. It was a nice piece of work to put the bristles on so they would stay. This we could do to perfection. If they came off they could not be put on again.

We made our shoe pegs of maple and dogwood, well seasoned, sawed the length and size we wanted the pegs to be. We split off slabs the thickness to make square pegs, and shaved the slabs to make pegs sharp at one end. We used a stick with a notch against which we held the slabs and sharpened first one side and then the other. A strip of leather with a slit in it was fastened to the shoe board. We took two or three of the sharpened slabs and held them with the left hand against the leather which served as a lever for the knife, and with the point of the knife held to place by running it in the slit in the leather, we split off the pegs.

The crop we put in on Cowlitz Prairie turned out well, and we hauled it over early in the fall, or enough of it to plant and keep us until we grew our first crop on Chambers Prairie. The winters of 1845-6 and 1846-7 were very mild and pleasant. We made the rails to fence in land to protect our crops. We raised plenty of wheat, potatoes, peas, and other vegetables. We had wheat coffee and pea coffee and we could always change from one to the other. Boiled wheat and milk made an extra dish for supper.

Father and Mother were highly pleased with the country and they thought that there was no place like it, fat beef off the range in February and plenty of oysters and clams for the digging. One beef would give us sixty pounds of tallow, and in those days tallow was an important item.

The same spring of 1848, we built the log barn which stood for over half a century and finally had to be burned on account of its being unsafe for the stock. It was built similarly to those already described, except that this barn had five apartments, two for hay and grain, one for stalls, one for wagons, and one for threshing. It was a long, narrow barn, and all under one roof. The clapboards were put on with wrought nails from England. The sheeting was of logs, put on the right distance apart to use four four-foot boards.

Thomas and I had been looking forward and calculating to return to Missouri in two years to see our girls, that we had left behind us. In 1848 Mother received a letter from our old home, telling about what had taken place since we left, and among the news was the marriage of a certain young lady, and this had the effect of making me contented to remain on Puget Sound.

This was a sensible decision, for during the winter of 1847, Indians broke out and massacred Dr. and Mrs. Whitman and many others at the Mission, near Walla Walla. The people of

RECOLLECTIONS

Oregon raised a company of volunteers to subdue the Cayuse tribe, the only hostiles. They succeeded in bringing the leaders to justice. We, on Puget Sound, did not know about the trouble until it was settled. The Indians here were friendly and they were glad to have the Bostons—as they called the Americans—come. About this time gold was discovered in California, and Thomas and I got the fever to go, as brother James was there.

CHINOOK WOMAN AND CHILD

ANDREW JACKSON CHAMBERS

Indian War of 1855-1856

That which took place on Chambers Prairie, the later part of August and September, 1855 decided the settlers to build a place of refuge in case the Indians should attempt to execute their threats. Their mode of warfare was to attack the settlers at night, to plunder, and if possible, to exteminate the whites. Among many of the scares we had was one when John Chambers, who understood the Indian language well, overheard "Old Ben" (who had told him had come to live and die with him,) say, "Little John knew when he sold me this knife" (at the same time smoothing the blade) "that I would kill him with it." He did not know that John was within hearing. This so frightened John, and William Elders, that they came to my house without their guns. I heard the click of the gate, and sprang for my rifle, my only thought being "Indians!" They hurried out of sight, fearing I would shoot them, knowing my watchfulness for Indians.

I sent them back for their firearms. On their return we moulded bullets all night.

General Stevens was making treaties with the Indians that spring, and a short time after treating with the Indians west of the mountains, he and his party went east of the mountains to treat with Indians there. At this time a report was started among the Nisquallys that the "Bostons" (that was the name called the Americans; the Hudson's Bay Company and their servants, they called King George men,) were laying plans to collect all the Indians together and take them in a large ship to a country where it was always night. A great many of the Indians came to me to learn whether this report was true. It was hard to talk them out of the false notion and to get them to name the parties that had told them this tale. It was always "they," but no definite person or persons. The young Indian that was working for me came out and said the Klickitats were coming over to this side of the mountains and would kill all the "Bostons." He wanted Mrs. Chambers and me to go to Fort Nisqually. He said it was safe there, because this tribe would not hurt the King George men.

I went to the settlers on the prairie and we called a meeting the next day. We decided to build a stockade around a large barn I had put up that summer. This barn still stands here on my place. The shed and stockade were long since torn away. The settlers came in force, and in seven or eight days we had a stockade one hundred feet square and sixteen feet high, with guard houses at the opposite corners. It was built of fir logs eighteen feet long, and from ten to twelve inches in diameter. These logs were set just as close together as they could be, straight up and down in a trench three feet deep.

Each family, as it came in, took a certain portion of the barn and shed, that extended around the barn. They partitioned off kitchens under this shed with lumber I had on the place. There were thirty-two families sheltered here at one time, and we had just hauled the crop into the barn, too. As near as Mrs. Chambers and I can recall the names of those who were in the fort with us, the list is as follows:

Mr. and Mrs. Ike Hayes, Mr. and Mrs. John Hayes, Mr. and Mrs. Charlie Eaton, Mr. and Mrs. Marcus McMillan, Mr. and Mrs. William Yeager, Mr. and Mrs. William White, Mr. and Mrs.

ANDREW JACKSON CHAMBERS

Tyrus Hines, Mr. and Mrs. Captain Tyrril, Mr. and Mrs. James Phillips, Mr. and Mrs. Stephen Ruddell, Mr. and Mrs. James Pattison, Mr. and Mrs. Archibald McMillan, Mr. and Mrs. A. W. Stewart, Mr. and Mrs. Thomas J. Chambers, Mr. and Mrs. David J. Chambers, Mr. and Mrs. Sam Wilson, Mr. and Mrs. Spurgeon, Mr. and Mrs. Stephen Guthrie, Mr. and Mrs. Abijah O'Neil, Mr. and Mrs. Joseph Conner, Mr. and Mrs. Joe Bunton, and Mrs. James McAllister and family.

The single men were as follows: Mr. Mayhard, Nathan Eaton, George McAllister, William Ruddell, William White, Rolland Wood, John Chambers, McLain Chambers, Henry Parsons, William Parsons, Joe White, Columbus White, Milton White, L. D. Barnard, Jonathan Prince, Levi Prince, Joseph Deaves, Joseph Guthrie, Sanford Guthrie, William Pattison, Nathan Pattison, Charles Pattison, John Pattison, and James Burnes.

While we were at work on the stockade, "Old Nanyumpkin" or "Stahi," used to come out on the prairie and watch us building. I think our making this stockade was the only thing that saved us. The Indians saw that we had means for protecting ourselves.

I can't remember just when the first scare came, but I know that thirty families gathered here at the fort within twenty hours after James McAllister was killed. He was killed close to Puyallup while returning as an express to acting-governor Mason. The soldiers had sent him with reports to the governor. Abraham Moses and Dr. James Burnes were with him, and some others whom I cannot recall.

RECOLLECTIONS

As soon as the fort was completed, a company was organized with Isaac Hayes as captgain, and A. J. Chambers as first lieutenant. I may state here, although the stockade was on my place, we stayed in it only a few nights. Mrs. Chambers preferred to stay in our house just outside the stockade, and thereby avoided the crying of children, the barking of dogs, and the scolding of the women. My young sister, Letitia, kept her company. Letitia said there were forty or fifty children, and thirty dogs in the fort. I volunteered to protect the homes of the settlers, and I would not be sworn into the United States service, because most of the volunteers were sent out of the country in pursuit of hostile Indians, leaving us unprotected at home. Some were disposed to think as I did, while others, who had nothing to live on, wanted to be sworn into the United States service to get rations. Nothing was said about taking this step until after the fort was completed, so it was fully a month after the company was formed before any entered the regular service.

I desired to protect the country and was scouting with that in view. Captain Hayes ordered me to select ten men but would not press horses into service. I chose James Guthrie, Rolland Wood, Sanford and Joseph Guthrie, Abijah O'Neil, William Ruddell, Marcus McMillan, McLain Chambers, Charlie and Nathan Pattison..Others were with us at that time who wished to visit their stock. We were busy riding over the settlement until late in December. I was often in the saddle three weeks at a time. On one of our scouting trips, some of the boys were very anxious to press horses into the service. On my father's place in Pierce County, he had a corral for horses. The boys ran some horses into this corrall and began selecting the animals, some of them taking two apiece. I asked them what they were doing. They answered, "Why, we might as well have these horses as for the Indians to get them." I told them we were out to protect the property of people, and I made them turn the horses out.

Because I would not press horses into service, I thereby incurred the Captain's displeasure, and during my absence on a third scouting trip, he called a meeting and elected William White to the position of first lieutenant. On my return, I called on Secretary Mason, acting governor, and told him what had occurred. He told me to continue in my position, and he would see that I was righted.

In consequence of my having incurred the displeasure of Captain Hayes, my name was never mentioned in any of the reports. I was not aware of this until about three years ago, when the questions of pensions was being discussed. I have affidavits of men who served with me.

We scouted the country until Joseph White's company came in from Puyallup and reported that the Indians were est of the river.

Two of the young Indians stayed on the prairie when their tribe went to the hostiles on the Puyallup River. Before the Indians left Chambers Prairie and vicinity, they cached their provisions. These two young Indians, wishing to show their friendliness, showed us where the caches were. We destroyed the provisions. Some of the folks were afraid these Indians were spies, and it was thought best to send them to Chehalis, the Indians there being friendly to the "Bostons."

RECOLLECTIONS

In traveling over the country a short time after this, we came upon an Indian family. They were friendly. We disarmed the man and sent a guard with the family to the Chehalis tribe. Mr. Sidney Ford, who was agent for the Chehalis tribe, succeeded in keeping them friendly.

About the latter part of December, the settlers became restless, and began to build block houses at different places, and two or three families went together so as to make preparations to plant a crop for the next year.

One man, Jim Burnes, did not want to remain on the prairie, although he had been sworn into service. The scouts found him plowing in a field near Yelm, with a gun strapped on his shoulder. They brought him back to the stockade, and locked him up in the block or guard house. Before they took him, he dropped his gun in the field and plowed it under. Some of the scouts wanted to put a rope on him and make him walk to the stockade, but he made them furnish him with a horse. The guards had become lazy about the fort. They wanted to bring this man in and make him stand guard. They did not realize that he was doing just as much good where he was.

Nathan Pattison was set to guard him, and while Burnes was talking away to his guard one day, he was at the same time digging for his liberty, and he was out and gone before any one suspected his purpose.

Mr Stephen Ruddell and Tyrus Hines built a block house on Mr. Ruddell's place; Mr. David Chambers and Mr. Wood built one on David Chambers' place; A. J. Chambers, Thomas Chambers, and John M. White built two block houses on A. J.

Chambes' place; John N. Lowe built one on his place and a family was taken in to help guard his place.

Mr. Connor and family, Mr. William White and family, Mr. O'Neil and family, Mr. A. W. Stewart and family, and Marcus McMillan and family built a block house on Nathan Eaton's place. These were all constructed to enable the settlers to put in crops, so that they would have provisions for the ensuing year.

The latter part of February, 1856, William Northcraft was waylaid and killed about two miles east of Chambers Prairie, while hauling supplies to the volunteers. On the 2nd of March, 1856, William White was killed at the east end of Chambers Prairie. About this time, Samuel Wilson was shot and wounded, and Glasgow's barn was burned. No one can imagine the desolation of the country when it came to the killing of these white men, for everyone thought the Indians had gone east of the mountains.

These depredations seem to have been committed by three Indians who had gotten around the volunteers and to the front of them. It was just about this time, too, that Governor Stevens had asked help from the Oregon volunteers, who had successfully quelled an uprising of the Indians in Southern Oregon. The Indians had stolen three horses and were leaving the country when the Oregon volunteers, camped at the blockhouse on Lowe's place, with Nathan Eaton as guide, came up and fired on them, and captured their horses. The Indians took to the woods. I don't think they ever reached their friends. This was the last that was ever seen of hostile Indians in this part of the country during the war. The last battle was fought in June, 1857, at or near Grand Ronde Valley, Oregon.

RECOLLECTIONS

Customs of Doctoring and Burial and
Religious Beliefs of the Indians on
Chambers Prairie in 1848.

The Indians believed in a supreme ruler, whom they called Caghalie Tyee, and in an evil spirit, whom they called Masa Tyee.

In the fall of 1848, Cataammouth, the great tamahnous of Chambers Prairie, had a patient, a young squaw, who had consumption. His mode of treatment was upon the presumption that she had an evil spirit. She lay near a large fire which was kept burning in the middle of the wigwam. Beside the fire was a basket of water into which hot stones were dropped to keep the water up to a certain temperature. A slab of wood as long as the wigwam would accommodate was so placed that singers could be seated on each side, and with small sticks to pound on the slab, making the most noise possible in perfect time to the chant which they sang.

When everything was ready, the doctor, who was leader in the chant, explained the nature of the disease, and then led off with the singing—all pounded the slab in rhythm. After keeping this up for a while, the doctor called a halt, and if their sticks were up in the air, they did not touch the slab, so powerful was his influence over them. He then explained to them how he was progressing with the patient, then they proceeded as before.

After a time, he placed his lips over the place where the disease was located, and determined to draw it to the surface, or into his mouth. He then went through a great many maneuvers and contortions, and chanted long and loud. After two or three hours of this work, he had a most desperate time, and then announced that he had succeeded in getting the evil spirit out of the woman.

35

ANDREW JACKSON CHAMBERS

He had a hard time to hold the spirit, judging by the many shapes into which he got himself. He finally plunged his hands into the basket of hot water, twisting them and making all kinds of contortions, and mashing the something all to pieces. He then opened his hands and blew the evil spirit into the fire.

This proceeding was kept up three or four hours each day and night and sometimes for weeks at a time, until the patient got well or died.

These Indians thought that if you had a hard time here and had to work, you would have an easy time in the next world. An Indian told me that as I had been good to him and had given him work here, he would give me work in the next world.

These Indians had three great tamahnous men, powerful doctors, who had great power over the common Indians. The Indians believed these doctors could come back in the shape of dogs and kill any one, and that it was impossible to escape from them.

If however one of their doctors failed to cure, and lost three or four patients in succession, they called a meeting of their tribe, and selected one of their number to shoot the tamahnous man, believing that the doctor had mesachie tamahnous (the devil in him.)

Once, when there was a case of the killing of one of these doctors, the selection fell upon a young Indian who was working for me. The doctor had told the tribe that a bullet would not penetrate his flesh. The young Indian said, however, it went into him just the same as it would into any other man.

RECOLLECTIONS

The Nisqually tribe buried their dead above the ground, sometimes in the trees. The greatest doctor of this tribe, Cataammouth, made arrangement as to his burial, with my father. He wanted stakes to be driven into the ground, leaving them two feet high. He wanted a box to be made, his body placed in it, and the coffin put on top of the stakes. When he died, my father had him buried according to agreement. The Indians brought his best horse and shot him beside the grave. They brought buckets and pans, and all his cooking utensils, punched holes in them, and hung them around the grave. The tribe intended to kill a squaw, one of his slaves, to attend him and wait upon him in the next world, but she ran away and remained in hiding in the woods for several days. Finally she came to my father, and he prevailed on the tribe not to kill her. That was the last on the Prairie of killing slaves to go with the dead.

When we were moving from Oregon to Chambers Prairie in the fall of 1847, we often came across canoes, canims, the Indians called them—with dead bodies in them. The canoes would not hold water. Sometimes they were stuck in the forks of trees along the river bank. These were always above the high water mark.

On the Columbia River, above the Cascade Falls, Memaloost Island was covered with canoes where the dead Indians were buried. No one was allowed to be buried there who did not own a canoe. It was considered an honor to be buried there among the Tyees.

One white man, Vic Trevitt, an Oregonian, requested that his body should be buried there. I have seen his grave. Memaloost means dead.

Andrew Jackson Chambers.

The Elizabeth White Chambers *Reminiscences* was written in 1894 but not printed until 1903, some nine years later. The text was dictated by Margaret White Chambers to Nora Chambers Hoskins. Publication was arranged by Elizabeth Chambers Hunsaker, presumably a daughter. A few copies were printed, particularly to give to children and grand-children. The Margaret White Chambers booklet is in consequence fairly rare, however copies are held by the Washington State Library (Olympia), Whitman College, Yale University and the Newberry Library.

Copies of the 1903 printing were formerly held by the University of Washington and Oregon Historical Society but both these institutions say their copies have disappeared. An eastern dealer had a copy for sale for two-hundred-fifty dollars.

Reminiscences

Margaret White Chambers

Ye Galleon Press
Fairfield, Washington
1975

REMINISCENCES

I left my childhood home in company with my three brothers, my sister-in-law, two nephews and a niece, on April 1st, 1851, to cross the continent with ox teams—no pleasant undertaking.

Never can I forget that morn when I bade good-bye to the dear old home, turned my back on all the familiar haunts of childhood, and bade old and dear friends and relatives a last farewell.

My only sister took the road leading to Louisville the same morning, having been married one week to Presly M. Hoskins. I can see the wagon yet that carried her goods, as it slowly turned down a hill that we used to travel so much to school and church together. Oh, how sorrowful a day that was!

We crossed the Wabash River at Terre Haute about twenty-five miles from our home in Sullivan County, Indiana. We traveled across Illinois and Missouri, landing at St. Joseph on the Missouri River the 9th day of May.

There we remained for a few days resting our jaded teams. The roads were very bad, in fact almost impassible, it being the spring of the year. At times the poor oxen would almost mire down.

I can't recollect the day of the month we left St. Joseph, but it was near the middle of May. One thing I do remember was my emotions after we were all landed on the Indian Territory side of the river. I felt as if we had left all civilization behind us. I don't remember anything of interest occurring for several days—not until we came to a stream called the *Little Blue*. It was overflowing its banks. There, we met a party of soldiers, a Major Wood and family with them, who had been east on a trip and were here water bound. (They were from Fort Laramie.)

As we had wagons, that were made to ferry our goods across streams, the Major wanted to hire my brothers to ferry them over. They took them across but refused pay. Major Wood was so pleased that he told them that anything we needed we should have if we called at the fort. My brothers thanked him and told him we were well supplied.

We had laid in a bountiful supply of provisions, for such a journey required a vast amount. None but those who have cooked for a family of eight, crossing the plains, have any idea of what it takes.

My sister-in-law was sick, my niece was much younger than I, and consequently I had the management of all the cooking and planning on my shoulders. I had my eighteenth birthday on the plains. How well I remember the day. We tried to make merry and have a jolly time.

Speaking of the cooking, there isn't much fun cooking with sage brush almost like straw—so dry. Sometimes the pan cakes (or flap jacks, as that was the more familiar name, being made from warm water and soda, and some sour dough, if one had it if not, we did without) I have turned over were black with the light ashes blown from the fire on them. You might ask, "Well, why didn't you throw them away?" Because the next one would, very likely, be just as bad, and we were very saving of the provisions.

REMINISCENCES

We had jolly times when we were all well. My brother's wife was sick most of the time, though. At one time we despaired of her life; but thanks to our Maker and Preserver, she was spared.

I used to think, when traveling over those rocky, rough roads, often seeing the skulls of fellowmen bleaching in the hot sun, so far from home and loved ones, that if we were spared to reach a land of civilization, I could see my dearest loved ones laid to rest without a tear. Oh, the thought of leaving a loved one so far away was perfectly agonizing.

We would often see parts of quilts that had been wrapped around the body of some dear one laid away, but both body and quilts had been dug out by the wild animals and the bones laid bare before the gaze of the pitiless sun.

We saw some graves that had been made secure by heavy stones being placed upon them so that the wild beasts could not roll them off.

We had one funeral in our train, a little boy, and how sad it was to drive away and leave the new made grave.

We had many experiences of different kinds—'twas a place to test human nature—the good and the bad will show for itself. I made some very dear acquaintances in traveling that proved to be good true friends.

We brought our dog. He was so attached to the whole family that we could not think of leaving him.

On the Platte River we had a very hard thunder storm, and, as he was always frightened so badly at home that we would run to the house for protection; there being no house to run to, he ran away and was gone for three weeks, when some parties came up with us one day, and said the company back of us told them our dog was with them. We had passed this company and they had seen the dog and knew him.

My brother and nephew rode back several miles and came up with the dog just as we had the evening meal ready, and what a rejoicing we had.

The poor beast was so glad that he would go first to one and then to another and lick their hands. His delight was greater than ours.

The poor dog perished in crossing the desert. We hauled water to do for two days, and on the second day, before we reached water, my sister-in-law being very ill, our minds were taken up with greater cares. We did not know if she would live until we could reach camp. I remember seeing the dog coming along behind our wagon, with his tongue hanging out of his mouth. Poor fellow! if he had been taken in and hauled a short distance and given a little water, he would have been all right. If we had had no sickness we would have looked out for the poor beast.

Except the sickness in our family we had an excellent trip, compared with some. We had no trouble with the Indians—only some scares.

One night the guards came in and said the Indians had frightened all the stock and they had run away. Of course we prepared to defend ourselves as best we could. The wagons were put around to form a circle, the tongue of one wagon resting on the back of the next. Then the women and children were put into as few wagons as possible and one man sat in front of each wagon, with his gun, ready to shoot if any Indian made his appearance. We were greatly rejoiced when morning came and not a sign of an Indian was to be seen anywhere. Some of the boys said the guards had become tired and perhaps scared, so they thought they would get up a little excitement.

Sometimes we would lay by all day and rest our poor worn out teams, when the weather was so warm. Then we would start out just at night fall and travel all night.

I missed the sight of the Court House Rock by passing it in the night. We had seen it at a distance for several days, rearing up like an immense old building. Chimney Rock, too, was quite a curiosity. We could see it for days, and it looked so close at hand, that three or four days before we got near it, some of the company started to go to it, but would come back into camp tired with walking a whole afternoon carrying their guns. The shape of the rock was very much like a chimney, standing alone way out on the plains with no other rock near.

We passed some very beautiful rocks very much like the ones in Yellowstone Park. On some of the smooth ones there were hundreds of names, each one higher than the last, the writers having climbed up to see who would write their names the highest.

The Devil's Gate is a queer freak of nature and is quite a curiosity. There is just room for a wagon road between the high rocks on either side. I don't remember their height.

We passed what was then called *Steamboat Springs*. The water was thrown up into the air several feet. It was a strange sight to see. Then there were the hot springs, some of the loveliest water-falls and so many, many other strange and beautiful things that I have forgotten now.

I have never seen any cactus here to equal those growing wild. Such beautiful flowers!

The most unpleasant part of the journey was through the alkali district. It was white as far as you could see. In some places a thick crust or scum was on top of the earth.

There were three deaths and one birth in our train. One death did not really belong to our company, but we took charge as the train the party belonged to had left them, they said they could not be detained.

Three of our women and three of our men stopped in Grand Round Valley with the poor old sick lady and her son and little girl. We left with the slow ox teams one morning, and she passed away that evening. They laid her to rest in what was then a wild Indian country, but is now a fine settlement, a beautiful and fertile country dotted with farm houses, and has two flourishing cities—Island City at one end of the valley and La Grande at the other.

The next evening our folks came up with us at camping time. They could travel much faster than we could with our poor, jaded, worn-out cattle.

Cows, as a general thing, stood the trip much better than oxen. We brought one yoke of young cows that we had milked at the home place, and more faithful creatures I never saw. They worked every day until in August, when coming through the Blue

Mountains, one of the poor creatures gave out and laid down and refused to get up; so we had to leave her and travel on. Our hearts were sad when we took a last look at one so faithful. We learned afterward that a company back of us found her quite refreshed after a rest, and brought her on through with them, which we were very glad to know. The two cows gave us plenty of milk until we reached the alkali country, then the feed was so poor that they had no milk for us.

This part of the road was the most unpleasant part of the journey, for the alkali was so thick that it formed a perfect crust, which, for miles, looked as white as snow. Our hands and lips were so sore from it. Such a dust as would raise as we traveled along. We would be so covered when we stopped at nightfall that we could not tell our nearest neighbors, as all looked alike.

Besides losing our cow in the Blue Mountains, we had another remarkable event—the birth of a son to Mr. and Mrs. Ross. (They and their son now reside in the Puyallup Valley.) The next day after the birth we laid by for half a day, then traveled on as though nothing had happened. Mrs. Ross and the baby got along nicely. She was able to take care of the baby in a short time and all went as smoothly as though nothing had occurred.

Think of the women now who have a doctor, a trained nurse and girl in the kitchen and then do not do as well.

The next event of importance was the ascension of the Rocky Mountains. It was a tiresome and tedious journey, and our cattle after traveling so far were very much fatigued. For days it was up, all the time and the road was often very winding. The five girls that were in our train would sometimes take what we called a "cut-off," and come in on the road a long distance ahead of the wagons. These five girls were Elizabeth White, now Mrs. D. R. Bigelow of Olympia; Jerusha White, now Mrs. A. W. Stewart of Puyallup; Millie Stewart, now Mrs. Dr. Spinning of Puyallup; Margaret White, now Mrs. A. J. Chambers of Olympia; and Mrs. Durgan of Olympia, whose maiden name is unknown.

One day, as we could see the road quite a distance off, we set out on one of our trips, which proved much longer than we had any idea of. We were climbing hills, tramping over rocks, through deep ravines and scattering timber all afternoon.

We caught up with a Mr. Skinner, after some hours travel, and we were glad, I can tell you, not that we were afraid at the time, but after thinking of the risk we ran of possible capture by the Indians, we became nervous and refrained from taking those short cuts unless we could see just how far we had to go.

About as "blue" a time as we had, was when our cattle were poisoned—every one lying down and groaning like sick people. Luckily for us, my brother had taken along a much greater quantity of bacon than our guide had recommended, so we had enough fat meat to let the entire company have some. The men sat up all night and cut the meat in such sized pieces as they could put down the throats of the animals; consequently our teams were saved and we were able to resume our journey the next afternoon.

The trials and troubles of such a journey can't be imagined by the uninitiated. I think that if the people of that day had realized the dangers and privations attendant upon such a trip, they would never have undertaken it.

I shall never forget the first herd of buffalo I saw. Such a number of them—perhaps a hundred. We often saw small herds traveling towards water.

The first meat was a great treat, as we had been so many months without any fresh meat. The boys in our company killed three one day, and we laid by a day and a half and dried some. We made a scaffold of sticks, and hung the strings of meat on the sticks, and then built a fire under the meat.

After this, when we wished to have a change from eating the dried meat, we would put grease in the pan and fry the meat just a short time. I can tell you we relished it after having lived for months on salted meat.

I shall never forget how good the first new potatoes tasted. We got them in Powder River Valley.

One sees the most beautiful wild flowers in crossing those wild plains—(as was then the familiar name to all the emigrants)— flowers of very hue and shade and acres of them. One place, Ash Hollow, on Burnt River, I remember particularly. The hillsides were complete masses of flowers. Oh, how I do regret not pressing and keeping some of the beauties; but that is a little thing to regret doing compared with the many things we look back and see as we journey on through life. So much occurs to us that we wish we had done.

MARGARET WHITE CHAMBERS

I think that nothing more of interest occurred until we reached The Dalles on the Columbia River. How very glad we were when we came to that point in our trip, for we knew we were nearing the journey's end, and also nearing civilization once more, where we could have the privilege of church and schools.

I had the first evening's encampment in this place stamped on my memory never to be blotted out from it, for I carry the scars today of a burn I got in preparing the first meal. As it was sandy all about here and high winds prevailed, we were under the necessity of digging a pit to build our fire in. As I was putting something over the fire to cook, the sand gave way under my foot and I came down with my hand in the hot sand and ashes, burning it to a crisp. That fixed me so that I could act the lady for some weeks.

The next morning, September 16, we took passage in a little steamer that plied between The Dalles and Cascades. It had just been built and this was its first trip. Here my sister-in-law met an old acquaintance, a Mr. Chenowith. How rejoiced she was! He was an engineer on the boat and was so kind to us. He would have us go to the table and eat. The boat did not furnish meals. Every one brought lunch, and we had prepared plenty, but that would not do; we must eat with them.

A short time after leaving The Dalles we heard there was a sick woman aboard. Pretty soon we found her, a woman in confinement. She was a stranger to us but two of our company's women attended her. She got on nicely, and when we reached the Cascades she was taken off, as the boat made daily trips.

Her husband was a *brave* fellow! When she was taken sick he *fainted*! The men had to get water and dash it into his face. With all, we had quite an interesting time.

We remained over night at the Cascades. There my brother who accompanied us purchased a flat-boat and we loaded into it and started for the mouth of the Sandy River, quite a distance from the Cascadaes.

My other two brothers, with two nephews and the rest of the men, drove the cattle down the trail on the Columbia, and a hard old time they had, too.

When we reached Sandy we found quite a nice farm house and a good garden of vegetables, which I can tell you looked inviting after nearly six months on dried beans, rice, bacon, dried apples and peaches. Although we had so little change in diet, yet we had cause for great thankfulness, as we had an ample supply and some to spare, which was more than many could say. Some were very scarce of provisions, but none were in want in our train.

Here (at Sandy) we camped on the banks of the Columbia, and my brothers took the contract of building a ferry-boat for the man that lived there. His name was Parker. He had a wife and only one child, a son. These people amused us very much sometimes. We took vegetables on my brothers' work. When we would ask her for cabbage, the old lady would say, "Have one head or two?" Our reply would be "Two, as we will take one apiece!" You would have supposed they were scarce by the way she would speak, but to the contrary, acres of all kinds of vegetables, and any number of heads of cabbage going to waste—all bursted open— but that is the style of some people.

Mr. Parker used to come to our tent and spend the evening chatting with us about our trip, and telling many interesting incidents of his experience. He had been several years in the country.

When the old lady Parker was ready to retire she would come to the door and call "Davie! Davie, come to bed or I will shut the door and lock you out," and if her husband did not answer, (as he was not likely to, if in a very interesting story) she would give the door a slam which would resound for some distance, and then all was quiet. We never knew if the old gentleman slept out on those nights or not.

Well as I had a sore hand, I was not much use when washing was to be done, and, as you may guess, we had not small amount of soiled and *more* than dirty clothes, after so long a trip, although we had washed every time we had an opportunity. It took my niece several days to complete the wash, as she had no help.

My memory fails me in regard to the length of our stay at this place, while waiting for the men and boys to come with the cattle. I think it was two weeks, perhaps more. Anyway when they did come we were very glad to see them.

The boat being finished, the cattle and goods were ferried over the Columbia, and then our *precious selves* were taken over. I shall never forget the fear I had of the Columbia. 'Tis an ugly stream! Many days in traveling from The Dalles to the mouth of the Sandy River, we would be compelled to lay by on account of rough water. The wind blew most of the time, but, as a general rule, it would calm down about sunset. Then we would travel the greater part of the night. We (the girls and women) would sleep while floating down the great river.

Our train separated when we reached The Dalles. Some went to Oregon City, some to Portland, some here and some there.

We found a very nice settlement on the river bottom after crossing over. Here, my brother and his wife stopped to take care of the stock, as there was an abundance of pasturage to be had very reasonably. My other brothers and two nephews, my niece and myself went to a little town between Portland and Oregon City, Milwaukie. There we rented a house and we girls tried house-keeping and going to school for a while. We enjoyed the winter quite well, considering we were among strangers and in a strange land; but God is everywhere, and through all our long journey we were protected and cared for, and watched over by that Loving Eye that never slumbers or sleeps.

Some of the young men found employment in Portland in the saw mills, my cousins and brothers among them. Altogether there were about half a dozen of them, and often on Saturday afternoons they would get a row-boat and come to Milwaukie and spend the evening and Sunday with us. There was an attraction for one young man, as my niece was his best girl and was finally his wife. Well we did have jolly times. There were several good singers among them and we would spend the evenings singing, and talking over our long trip.

We soon made some very pleasant acquaintances, as all were new comers and it was a small town. We attended singing school, and some few dancing parties, *only* to look on. I had never seen nor heard a violin before nor seen any dancing. My people were all very strict Presbyterians and we were never allowed to indulge in such amusements.

In December, my brother and his wife came to us, as he wanted to find a suitable place to locate and did not like the place where they had been with the cattle. He found a place east of Milwaukie about five miles. He cleared a small area, built a small house of logs, and in March moved out on it, my niece and self accompanying them. My other brothers and nephews looked around somewhat and finally went to the mines in California.

We had no snow that winter until March, and then the snow and rain came down every day during the month. Some days the sun would shine nice and warm and melt all the snow away. Then the clouds would gather and the rain and snow would come again. I shall never forget how dreary the woods looked as I had never been used to evergreen trees in winter. Now I think it a grand sight to see them in their robes of white after a fall of snow.

We remained on this place with my brother until July and then we girls thought we would like to earn something for ourselves. We went to Portland. I found a nice place at Rev. Horace Lyman's, the first Congreational minister of that place. He came as a missionary. He had a wife and one little girl. It was there I first earned money. My niece had a very good place with a Dr.

Warren's family. Here we had the privileges of church services and society, of which we were deprived in the country.

In September my brothers came to the Sound to see if they liked the country better, as we were not favorably impressed with Oregon. As they were pleased they returned for us, and we all came to this part of the country, Chamber's Prairie, Thurston County, in October of 1852.

We spent the winter at the eastern extremity of the prairie, on the place where the widow Collins now lives, but which was owned by Mr. Nathan Eaton at that time. My brothers did the first fencing he had done on the prairie. They put in grain on shares and looked around for claims. My two brothers and a nephew took donation claims adjoining each other. They had not remained in California long.

The latter part of the winter of 1853, my brothers split and sawed all the lumber for our houses, as sawmills were then unknown in this part. We had puncheon floors. For fear you will not know what this is I will tell you. It is a floor laid with split logs, the flat side being uppermost. The logs were of cedar and the floor was *so* nice and white when scrubbed with sand and cold water. We girls used to be very proud of our white floors. I think it was in April, 1853 that we moved into our new home. We girls were the house-keepers for my brothers and nephews. My married brother lived a mile from us, on the place where Mr. Stralehm lives now.

That summer was a very dreary summer to us as we had never been where there were forest fires. I shall never forget our fears and anxiety of mind, thinking that the fire might come on us any time, as the grass on the prairie was very thick and dry. For days the sun hung like a ball of fire in the heavens. When the rain came the smoke cleared away and all was pleasant. We soon forgot our disagreeable times.

Our house-keeping for my brothers was of short duration, as my niece made up her mind to be some one elses house-keeper; so early one morning in September, the 22nd, of 1853, she was married to Mr. A. W. Stewart, a young man who crossed the "Plains" with us. After her departure I made my home with my brother and his wife until January, 1854.

On the 18th. of that month I was married to Andrew J. Chambers and came to reside in this house. We have spent our lives since then here and by the laws of nature we haven't many more years to live; but I hope we shall live them here, where we have seen our greatest joys and sorrows. I must say that I had never known what true happiness was until I was married, as I had never known the love of father or mother. I found great happiness in a loving affectionate husband. I only hope that all my daughters might be as happily united in marriage as their mother. We have raised a large family of girls, (that we are more than proud of) ten in number, seven living, of whom five are married and two are home to cheer our declining days, although the youngest is still in school.

The Indian War of 1855 and 1856 was a trying time on the new settlements. About as badly frightened as I have ever been in my life was during the fall of the Indian War, before the outbreak of the Indians. They had acted very strangely, and we had frequently heard rumors that the Indians east of the mountains were coming to take the country, and not a hint that those on this side had any hostile intentions.

We had an Indian boy working for us, and he thought a great deal of us. He told us again and again that he wanted to go to Fort Nisqually, the Hudson Bay Fort. One Sunday evening he came to us, all excitement, and told us that the bad Indians were coming in a short time and would kill all of us. My husband would not let on to him that we were afraid, so he went away looking as if he felt pretty bad.

A brother of my husband's lived a mile from us on the place his father settled on in 1848. This brother and a young man who lived with him were sitting outside their cabin late in the twilight one evening, in the hearing of the Indian camp. As they understood the Indian language and heard their names mentioned, they listened and heard the old Indian say, as he passed his fingers over the edge of a large knife he had bought from John Chambers: "Little did John think he was selling me the knife to kill him with." Then they talked and planned how they could execute their bloody work, and about this time the boys made tracks for our house, so scared they left their guns.

How well I remember that night! My nerves were very much shaken by the visit the Indian boy made us in the early evening.

When we heard the gate open and shut, Mr. Chambers sprang out of bed and grasped his gun. I tell you those boys made tracks when they heard him, for they knew he had his revolvers and gun ready. As soon as they could speak they called to him, and I tell you we were relieved when we heard who it was. Oh, how I shook! Just like one with the ague.

Then the men sat up on guard and ran bullets all night, as that was the only kind of ammunition we had in those days. We never closed our eyes all night and were very glad to see the day-light.

Early the next morning the boys returned to their homes to see how things looked. The old Indian was as fine as could be and wanted to be very gracious. He had told John Chambers some time before that he had come to camp by him and ws going to live and die by him. The old *hypocrite!* (The Indians are the most treacherous mortals on earth.) When he saw the boys he asked them where they slept. They replied, "In bed." "Not here," he said. Then they asked him how he knew. He said they were in the house to see if they hadn't some medicine for a sick child, which was another story.

Very soon we heard of men being waylaid and shot and the country was all excitement. Shortly the people began to gather into the forts to protect themselves. The fort for this part of the country was on our place and is till in use as a barn. There were block houses on each corner. At one time there were thirty-two families in this fort. There were any number of children and dogs, and consequently, any amount of music, especially evenings. It was rather amusing to hear the babble of so many voices. It was almost equal to the confusion at the Tower of Babel.

REMINISCENCES

We had many startling events, of which, I remember one well. My husband was Lieutenant of the company of volunteers in the fort, so he was ordered by the Captain of the company to take a number of men and make a scout through the country and see if any Indains were prowling around.

They mounted their horses about five o'clock one afternoon and rode hastily away toward the Yelm Prairie. Shortly afterwards the command was given for every man to get his gun and stand in readiness as the Indians might attack the fort at any moment, as they had undoubtedly attacked the men who had gone on the expedition, for they had heard the report of several guns in the direction they had taken.

Such a commotion! My feelings could better be imagined than described; but time told us our fears were groundless.

That was a long night; not a wink of sleep for me. Morning came but no signs of the Indians. The men were out two days and never saw or heard of an Indian. How rejoiced I was when I saw my good husband again!

There was one man in the company who used to give us a scare by firing his gun when he was on guard. The orders were not a gun to be shot unless at Indians. Knowing this, imagine yourself, sitting by the fire with everything quiet, and then hear one shot after another. It was *enough* to frighten any one. The old man always said he saw Indians.

There is a great deal more that I could write but time will not permit me. The war broke out in October, 1855, and closed in June of 1856. The last battle was fought east of the mountains.

Margaret White Chambers

A SKETCH OF A MIGRATING FAMILY

TO CALIFORNIA IN 1848

A Sketch of

A MIGRATING FAMILY TO CALIFORNIA

in 1848

By

RICHARD M. MAY

YE GALLEON PRESS
FAIRFIELD, WASHINGTON

* Asterisk means word is filled in.

Library of Congress Cataloging-in-Publication Data

May, Richard M.
 A sketch of a migrating family to California in 1848 / by Richard M.
May.
  p. cm.
  ISBN 0-87770-494-5
  1. Overland journeys to the Pacific. 2. West (U.S.) -- Description
and travel -- 1848-1860. 3. May, Richard M. -- Journeys -- California. 4.
May family. 5. California -- Gold discoveries. 6. California - - Description
and travel -- 1848-1869. I. Title.
F593.M47   1991   917.804′2--dc20   91-13420

A SKETCH OF A MIGRATING FAMILY TO CALIFORNIA

We had everything ready on Sunday morning at 9 o'clock, May 7th, 1848 and moved forward to Nashville on the Missouri River and lay there two hours under the hospitable roof of G.S. Turtle when we embarked on board the steamer *Hayden* (S. Thomas, master and much of a gentleman) for Independence, Miss. We landed safe at the point on the 10th at 2 in the morning, at Wayne City from thence to Independence 2½ miles. I went on horseback and employed a Mr. Stowe to purchase a yoke of oxen and 2 wagons and other articles of outfit for which I paid him near $100. All things being collected together, we left Independence on the 12th of May, but previously dispatched a message to Joseph Childs who was at the head of a train for that distant land and informed him I was on the way who promptly sent me word that he would wait or travel slowly until I reached him. We left Independence and encamped at the end of 10 miles it being the first time in my life of ever seeing a tent spread in order to defend the wind and rain, it being enclosed all around. Nothing occurred until the 21st, occasionally a thunderstorm. On that day we had the joy and pleasure of arriving at Capt. Childs' who very kindly had us take supper with him. On the 22nd we traveled about 14 miles and near 2 o'clock passed the junction of the St. Joseph road. It rained all day and in the evening it fell in torrents. I just thought as I was driving the team along this is the sweet portion of traveling to California. This day one of my steers became weary and sullen and we turned him out. The next morning the 23rd I went back for my ox and found him. Still raining and the wind blowing very hard but having on my rain* cloak and cap did not suffer seriously. All hands are in camp today, laying too in consequence of the rain yesterday. The face of the country is most beautiful being destitute of timber and

5

water. It is one extensive prairie with now and then a narrow string of timber lining the banks of creeks. The Kansas is about 350 yards wide from bank to bank it being very low (fordable). We cross half its bed on a sandbar which tried the strength of the teams. This stream is about 100 miles from Independence on the Road to Oregon. The timber on the streams is very low and worthless. The soil will compare with any district of country in the Mississippi Valley. Kentucky not excepted and most beautifully carpeted over with luxuriant growth of grass, which gives our weary oxen a fine repast during the night. The road is as good as any I every traveled, some very deep ravines and some buttes that have rocks piled up on them to show the traveler the way to the far west. We made a good day's journey. On the 25th 3 yokes of oxen traveled forward 7 miles and by the time we got them into camp it was too late to move that day. The men generously helped me to find them. The 26th we traveled 12 miles and camped on the Blue near 300 miles from Independence the 28th we made 10 miles and encamped on the Blue. 29th we lay by all day, in consequence of an express coming on to Capt. Childs desiring to stop a day or two until they could overtake him. The 30th of May we traveled 12 miles and encamped on the Blue again. We saw several antelope yesterday and today but our sharp shooters could not take them with their rifles. I had forgot to mention that I found my oxen, 3 yokes of them forward on the road 7 miles again. I now stake the leader of nights and shall in all probability get clear of hunting them. We met yesterday and the day before 22 wagons from the mountains laden with buffalo robes and tongues principally. One train of 7 wagons belongs to Mr. Shaw who commanded the steamer, *Tobacco Plant,* who I had seen a few times on the river. Mr. Millington was in company with the train, who gave me a pair of mockisons and through Capt. Childs I received of them a piece of dried buffalo. I did not forget to requite them for their favor by giving them some coffee and sugar, a sufficiency to last them to the States. This evening late one of the company brought in an antelope and true to the life of a hunter, divided it with those that were journeying with him.

The 31st of May we traveled about 10 miles and encamped on Blue River. A young elk was killed today and a turkey. 1st June, we left Blue River today and made for the dividing ridge between Platte and Blue. Traveled about 12 miles, took up early. It has been a blustering day, the wind blowing a strong gale and rained in the evening. I find by experience that it requires some knowledge of cattle to get along in a train. An experienced driver has less difficulty than those unacquainted with the business of driving. Our traveling community are all cheerful and in a good humor this evening although several tents were blown to the ground. We number, men, women and children, 112 and of that number these are 37 men and we are in hourly expectation of being overtaken by a train of 18 wagons and 12 men with pack mules.

The landscape on the Blue River is delightful, the lowlands being as level as a bowling green and as rich as could be wished. The high prairie is undulating and every way calculated for agricultural purposes. The great amount of timber will prevent its settlement for many years. In traveling up Blue River in all the branches we crossed emptying into it we found coarse sand and gravel and seldom any water in them. The prairie all the way to this point is handsomely decorated with wild flowers which would give a botanist employment and diversion.

The dull monotony of a prairie journey is quite tiresome, it being so very uniform that the variety we seek is nowhere to be found. The crack of the whip the clanking of chains and the still more disagreeable shriek of wagons is all that the sense of hearing conveys to the mind. Now and then the lark and quail* will give you one of their best and sweetest notes to cheer* you while journeying in these endless prairies.

We encamped four miles from Blue River, 2nd June we traveled 14 miles and encamped on the Nebraska or Platte River where we lay. We did not get a good view of it, our encampment being on a slough about 180 yards wide. Just before we reached this river we passed the bluffs that show the line of the river very distinctly for many miles to the right and left. These bluffs are composed of sand and clay sufficient to grow a fine award of grass and is about 2½ miles from the margin of the river. The intervening lowland is as rich as the Missouri bottoms in the central part of the State of Missouri.

Where we lay, ⅔ of Grand Island lies below (so said by those acquainted with it) 4⅓ above. Our course is up this river a little south of west.

3rd of June. We traveled about 12 miles and encamped on the same slough. Today we passed 4 companies of the Oregon Battalion. They were laying off a fort, the point being selected heretofore. The tended field in the open prairie had quite an imposing appearance. The train of government wagons, 23 in number, 12 of which were employed in transporting artillary and the fixtures belonging to the camp.* This new fort is about 200 miles from Fort Kearney and that Fort being 155 miles from Independence, gives you the distance we are on the way to the distant west.

I have lived to see one Pawnee Indian. He came into camp this morning begging something to eat. We fed him and no doubt he would steal all my property tonight if he could.

The Nebraska River puts me in mind very much of the Missouri River, its waters being muddy and rolls and boils in the same way. The current not quite so rapid. (The fort spoken of is to be called Childs).

4th June. We lay in camp. Nothing transpired worthy of note.

5th June, 1848. This day we traveled near 12 miles up the Nebraska on our course. I rode out to the margin of the river today and had a fine view of it. I would suppose the river to be 1½ miles in width. Its waters are turbid and rolls and boils very much like the Missouri. I also took a short hunt into the sand hills for antelope. Found plenty of game but killed none.

Those sand hills are worthy of a remark. It will be recollected that they form the bluffs on either side of the river. They have the appearance of a succession of mounds, one rising above another and covering 1½ miles wide running parallel with the river. The whole adjoining country appears to be under the influence of these hills at any rate the sand blown for miles from these hills has given character to the soil as the Nebraska has given character to the Missouri River.

Major Hensley arrived in our camp this evening, he being one of a mule train that I spoke of some two or three days ago.

June 6th, traveled 12 miles. Early this morning one of the company and myself repaired to a newly thrown up mound with a spade dug 3½ feet and found an Indian buried there. He has his implements of war and of taking game in his arms, laying on his right side with his head to the north. This evening 15 or 20 of us repaired to a small mound and dug some 5 feet and found a great many bones and in one of the joints of his spine was a spear which had punctured to the spinal marrow. His head and under jaw was found entire with most of the teeth. In both instances we carefully put the implements in the grave and filled it up.

June 7th. Made 16 miles today and in the evening had a fine thunder storm which is of common occurence on the Platte. It has been very cool so that coats and pants were quite agreeable during the last few days.

June 8th. Moved 12 miles today, the morning very cool and a strong gale of wind from the north. A great deal of complaint in camp too, though I think none of it is serious. The sand hills on our left are getting quite ragged and show the line of our journey while the great Nebraska rolls on in silent sublimity on our right. Capt. Childs killed a fine buffalo and generously divided among the company. Late this evening the emigrant wagons were* just below us on the river. I met in that company Daid and John Plummons who once lived in Cole County, Mo. The only gentleman I have seen since I left Boone County that I was acquainted with, that were traveling to the far west.

9th June. We made 20 miles today and have plenty of buffalo meat in camp having killed four today. We make quite a show after receiving 18 wagons more to our train. The number now is 47 (wagons), near 80 men, quite a formidable force. The sand hills have neared the river. A great portion of the road today has been on the most beautiful slope for cultivation I every beheld. I will just remark that when we have any road as bad as roads in the States I will mention it.

10th June. Made 15 miles today. We have been 7 days on the Nebraska and make the crossing tomorrow if nothing prevents. The greater portion of this days travel was crossing the spurs of sand hills which formed a beautiful slope or inclined plane facing the north, highly calculated for agricultural purposes so far as soil is necessary. We passed the forks of the river today. We have been in Buffalo

Range several* days and seen some thousands of them feeding at large on this entire prairie country. There is scarcely a tree or shrub in sight of encampment. I have just returned from the digging of a well. It affords a sufficiency of water for us all. It is common to dig wells on this river and we never fail to get water. It is always quite good. Several buffalo have been killed and we have plenty of fresh buffalo which makes a most delicious supper for a wagoner, and a very green one at that.

A considerable band of buffalo crossed our path today, so near as to endanger our teams remaining fast to the wagons so we loosed them and fired the rifles, without effect.

June 11th. Traveled 10 miles today and crossed the south fork of the Nebraska or Platte, both meaning the same, vis: Broad and flat. We have found grass very short since we reached the Buffalo range. The whole country seems to be grazed down by the Red Man's cattle. On our present encampment the grass is very good. The South Fork is near three fourths of a mile wide and from one to 2½ feet deep. It required about four hours to cross the stream with 47 wagons, having to double the teams to each wagon, thereby giving our oxen two trips across this broad flat river. No timber except a tree now and then on an island. Willows and Buffalo chips make our firewood. I will not anticipate our journey tomorrow as I did yesterday.

Changing sides of the river has changed our position. The sandhills on the right and the river on the left. I can now believe the buffalo stories so often told having seen whole sections of them on either side of the river. We had a fine piece of buffalo veal for the last two meals and now have a fine quarter of a heifer which I expect is much more substantial.

June 12th. Traveled 12 miles. This morning early while all

hands were gearing up teams a very large old buffalo run into camp. Capt. Childs fired on him while running and gave him a deadly wound. Men, women and children had to take a look at the monster. We geared up and moved one or two miles and a band of buffalo broke in upon us from the sand hills and very much alarmed the women. The men made a sally and defended with great effect felling one and wounding several deadly. Hooked on our teams, onward and westward we moved. The ground over which we passed has the mark of desert* although well coated vegetation. The sand and pebbles showing very near the surface. I will just remark here that in our company there are more general intelligence than I have ever seen developed in the same number of men in any community I was ever acquainted with. Willows for firewood and buffalo chips.

13th June. Traveled 15 miles over quite a fertile country. This day has brought with it great lamentation. One of the emigrants rode out into the sand hills yesterday to a short hunt and did not get in last night and it caused some concern. This morning 10 or 12 men took a look for him and have returned without seeing any sign of him, which has created great excitement. The lost gentleman is by name Peterson. Should he not get in he will be a great loss to the train and still greater to his wife and children. He was from Lafayette County, Mo. Mr. Peterson had endeared himself to me from the pleasant manner in which he helped me to find my cattle when strayed away.

About dark the lost gentleman got into camp and gave us much jabber, and his family still more.

14th June. Made 15 miles over a tolerable bad road and in its character. Have seen but few buffalo during today.

15th June. We laid on the south bank of the south fork of

Platte River all day. It is a little amusing to see how the willows are brot to camp for wood. We take a mule or horse which always has a long rope tied to his neck, then cross a slough into an island, cut the willows make them fast to the rope, then make the rope fast to the horn of the saddle, then into the slough, thence to camp. This is the way we make fires to cook and wash. The buffalo grass is blue looking grass and equal to the blue grass of the States. It is very short but very rich in nutriment. We have passed many dog towns, spoken of by writers hereto fore. The little animal is a clay color about the size of a squirrel, though not of the same make, being more bunchy. I will here give an outline of the route to Fort Hall. We shall leave this point, say 45 miles above the forks for the North fork tomorrow, thence up that part Fort Laramie to near the mouth of Sweet Water River, thence up that stream to the very head, thence through the south pass, thence across Bear River, thence to Fort Hall on Lewis River. I have been thus particular that if this journal should fall into any ones hands that has never traveled the road, he may anticipate the route before him.

The lads and lassies had a dance on the plains this evening.

16th June. We made 20 miles which places us on the North fork the bluffs have a wild romantic appearance. The river has a much stronger current than the south fork. The grass is poor and just in keeping with the country which we traveled over.

17th June. Moved 15 miles through heavy sand the greater part of the distance.

18th June. Traveled 22 miles and passed 2 Indian villages of the Sioux Nation. Come in sight of the Chimney Rock.

19th June. Passed the Chimney Rock and traveled 24 miles, a hard day's drive.

20th June. Traveled 30 miles, a still harder day's drive. Passed

Scott's Bluff. We drove until midnight and in passing over a small branch of Horse Creek broke the reach* of Capt. Childs' wagon. We came to a dead halt at that late hour without wood, the cooks continued to sleep for all had gone to sleep except the wagoners. I shall hereafter style myself the wagoner for the sake of variety.*

The country through which we passed for the last three days has the most romantic appearance of any my eyes ever beheld. The wagoner's language falls to describe the magnificent grandeur of the rocks and sand hills on the Nebraska. I have taxed my imagination to see if I could add another variety to the different shapes and figures presented to view, in particular on the North fork, but such is the sublime and picturesque scenery that I would as soon undertake to add another tinge to the rainbow.

I have intended to give my views as to the formation of the lowlands of the Nebraska. They are formed by the decomposition of the bluffs in part and also of the drifting sands from the hills. Then of course the formation is not primitive but secondary. It can be seen distinctly that where there is a great fissure in the bluffs there we find sand deep and heavy and yesterday we passed a place of this kind where there was a quantity of cedar and pine embedded in the sand. These bluffs are sparsely timbered with that kind of timber.

21st June. We drove from our midnight encampment and drove 2 miles and eat breakfast, then drove 5 miles and nooned, then 6 miles and encamped on the North fork, making 13 miles. The scenery very sublime. The Black Hills was in sight today from a very elevated situation. The grass is not so abundant as wished for.

22nd June. Traveled 20 miles and passed Fort Laramie. This fort is built on Laramie Fork of the North fork of the Nebraska, near 640 miles from Independence, Mo. It has the appearance of neatness above what I had anticipated. There was at this fort near

14

1000 Indians which annoyed us very much begging and stealing. Several of our surplus ox bows was stolen, hard wood being in demand. They made a demand upon our generosity as did other villages. We gave them a small quantity of tobacco, lead, beans, meal and flour and other things that were useful to them.

I will now give a short history of the one night in this Indian Territory. Beginning at the time we leave the road for water and ending in the road in the morning. The Capt. leads to the water at a distance ahead, when he reaches the intended encampment he turns his horse or mule broadside (as a signal) the gee haw go along as the case may be. The whip is cracked as a token of gladness. We arrived at the place, the foremost wagon drives around the ring and stops so as to be behind the hindmost, each man driving his wagon so as to stretch a chain from one wheel to another, there-by making a good fence by corraling. In the morning the morning guard drives in the cattle, yoke up boys and drive out and take your respective places in the road.

23rd and 24th June. Recamped 1½ miles above Fort Laramie. This fort I visited today and found it a quadrangular structure and built of dobies, viz, sun dried brick. It covers ½ acre of ground with sentry boxes on the corners and contains within a blacksmith shop and a stable sufficient for 30 horses, also various trading rooms one of the proprietors told me that they brought on 25,000 dollars worth of goods annually. I saw no mounted guns.* One small place was say 3 pounds was laying in a portico much neglected.

Mr. Burdien is now proprietor of this fort or trading post. About one mile below Mr. Risaw (formerly of St. Charles) is proprietor of another establishment of about the dimension, but in an unfinished condition. Just at the time I was in these forts trade appeared to be quite brisk, there being near 150 lodges of Indians.

Here the lame cattle were disposed of and all the wagons repaired that required it. An entertainment was given by Mr. Burdien this evening and several young ladies and gentlemen from the trains partook of his generosity. Dancing was the entertainment* resorted to on this occasion. This fort is 320 miles from the Santa Fe and 300 miles from the Missouri River. Fort Platt is the name of the other establishment just below, say 1 mile.

25th and 26th June. I visited the fort again and gave 5 lbs. of tobacco for one buffalo robe and 4 lbs. tallow. The tobacco cost me one dollar in the States and I sold it for $5.

27th June. This morning we rolled out from Laramie River and took to the black hills and hills they are. We had a very rough road to travel. At noon we came to a large spring 12 miles from the fort then traveled 8 miles further and encamped without grass for our oxen. We was (sic) in sight of high hills all day and I several times took it to be a cloud rising, it being in the west and very little to the left of our travel.

28th June. Left camp in a hurry so as to get to grass. Traveled 14 miles and came to the one thing needful. Here we met 10 men from Oregon, 7 out of the ten disliked the country and was returning home. The other three intended going back and said it was good enough for them. One gave us a bad account of the grass, saying it was all dried up this being one of the driest seasons almost ever known. The high land seen on our left turns out to be Laramie's Peak. The road has been very rough since we left Scott's Bluffs.

29th June. Traveled 8 miles and made a noon halt on the north fork of the Platte. The river has been in sight every few miles, but this is the first time we made a halt upon it. The scenery here is quite romantic and if there was any poetry in the Wagoner he would be bound to let a little of it but due and imperfect, prose is all he promises. The river issues here from a gorge in the hills and can be seen but a short distance. Vertical bluffs close it in suddenly. The current here is at the rate of six miles per hour. In all today we made 14 miles and encamped on the north fork. Poor grass.

The river just below entered a canyon and was lost to view by its serpentine course through the vertical rock which rose to 300 and 400 feet above the stream.

30th June. This day we made 15 miles and made no halt until the distance was traveled. We traveled up a mountain some 9 miles and headed a creek and dropped into another creek and encamped. The scenery very rich. To our left a line of low peaks were in sight. Scarcely a spear of grass to be seen but was perfectly dry.

We are now very near out of the rainy region, but it is thundering at this time. Still I do not anticipate the shower.

In traveling through a country like this the mind is naturally led to some conclusions as to the worth of it. Having neither timber, water nor soil you would suppose it worthless and so it is individually but it is of great worth to the United States. The furs, and necessaries of life taken in these mountains form a very considerable link in commerce which gives employment to a great number of her enterprising citizens. This morning at our encampment I picked up a piece of porous rock so light that it floated on water.

1st July. Traveled 18 miles, the teams under the yoke all the time. Today decidedly the richest scenery surrounded us that we have had the pleasure of seeing on the journey. We traveled through ridges* and gorges in the mountains, giving to us every variety of height from the snowy region down to a mole hill. In passing through a gorge we passed a confused pile of rocks 200 feet high appeared to have been thrown up by some powerful convulsion. The rocks laying in every form except a natural one. In view of our road the Buttes showed plainly. The dust is very bad today and is about the color of mader now and then some as white as snow. The buttes and hills generally about the color of dark ashes. The rocks are of all colors and of all sizes. What is generally called the Lost Stone of Missouri is here in abundance. Very little of the flat or round* rock to be seen in this region. The wild sage is the only shrub worthy of note. The branches have some cottonwood and boxelder timber, very short and worthless except for firewood. This country appears to have been in a volcanic state at some period or other from the appearance of the rocks and earth. In fact the whole face of it has a volcanic appearance.

2nd July. Moved 10 miles and halted for the evening. The scenery not so rich, but the road better. We met some twenty of pack mules and horses returning from Oregon. I had a few minutes conversation with them, but nothing worthy of note in the way of news.

The captain came in this evening having killed 3 buffalo. Several of the company killed game today.

3rd July, 1848. This has been a very warm day. Traveled 10 miles through quite a pleasant country to be in the mountains, the road good and very pleasant encampment. Everything has a cheerful appearance. The grass is a little too short for the cattle.

The wagoner intends to say something about the cattle soon. They are all doing tolerable well as yet. Some tenderfootedness manifested on their part and a great deal of solicitude on the part of their owners for their welfare. I have seen wagons mended in every way* in the States I thought, but our best mechanics cannot teach a mountainer a trick in doing up such things. Broke the tongue* of a wagon short off and in minutes the wagon is going. So with any other part of it. Fasten tires by driving wedges between it and the rounds. The dexterity with which wagons can be mended would astonish any person not acquainted with the art. Coarse canvass is the best fastening for boxes and should any of your spokes become loose in the hub canvass is the article to fasten them draw on your tire and all is right.

4th July. This day we all recollect as the anniversary of our independence and intend enjoying it by taking a buffalo hunt. The wagoner took a stroll up the creek to an encampment of about 20 Oregon gentlemen, rough and rude were their appearance, but their intellectual facultie were good and only parallel with all I have seen from that distant land. A Mr. Umphet returned to camp with me. I found him very social. He was returning to Ohio with the view of going to Oregon next spring. He also gave me some valuable information of that country. The hunters have returned and have plenty of buffalo beef, elk and deer, having killed 12 buffalos. Our camp was very well illuminated drying the meat. The manner of drying is very simple. Raise a scaffold about 2 feet high, lay small sticks close together across it, cut the meat in thin slices, then lay it on the sticks, the larger and thinner the pieces the better, build a fire under it so as to dry it in three or four hours. Be careful not to salt it at all. And should you have time and sunshine it will dry in that. It is very good. The Indians live on such meat all summer and in fact all the time it keeps well. I have eat of it dried last winter.

5th July. Traveled 15 miles and camped on the north fork again. Nothing of interest occurred on the travel. Just after we had stopped and while we were pitching our tents, a very pleasant hail storm passed over. You may depend upon it we were well prepared. The hail lay all night. We had some pleasure of drinking ice water.

The captain and two of his men failed to get into camp. There was some uneasiness manifested about them but knowing his familiarity with the mountains I could not be uneasy.

July 6th, Moved 6 miles and encamped 2 miles above the ferry. What, say, you, got a ferry 800 miles in the Indian country? Yes, sir, got a ferry and that kept by Mormons too. They charge $1.50 for crossing a wagon and its load.

The scenery at a distance is very beautiful. We have traveled parallel with a range of mountains on our left, the last hundred miles. Some of our men have gone to the ferry to help up with the boat. Our cattle are on good* grass. Tomorrow will bring something else.

7th July. Late evening the boat arrived near our encampment and all hands are busily employed in making ready to cross this turbid stream, with a strong current. The captain detailed 6 hands to dig down the bank on the other side or north bank. The wagoner was one of them. We found the grass* growing in all its native glory being three feet high and the roots formed a perfect mat in the sand. This being done our ferry boat began to ply. Our wagons began to land on the opposite bank at the rate of about 4 per hour. All got over except about 3 or 5. The Mormons who are stationed here (4 in number) are quite intelligent, and manly. The most of the emigrants in this train paid them in trade. I paid them in coffee at 25¢ per lb. The coffee which paid them cost me 8¢ per lb. Some wagons started for a new encampment. We followed up the river and we had not traveled more than 1½ miles before we split into two parties and now it might be said we are in four distinct companies. Where I turned in there was 9 wagons and the most beautiful encampment I have ever seen. On the north the hills put in very close while on the south the mountain heights are in full view.

At the same time the east and west is lined with a very dense growth of young cottonwoods. The little bottom of about 100 acres is covered with a fine award of grass. Indeed this rural spot has charms which make me forget my weariness. The birds are singing, bells ringing and children playing as if this was a civilized country. So we have pleasures in traveling through this district of America.

We have some sick, Mrs. Williams, a lady of fine accomplishments is very sick and in fact dangerously ill. Also Mr. McClellen lies prostrate and some doubt is entertained of his recovery.

The 8th of July we got the wagons over and ran up to our encampment, no accident happening whatever, the Mormons being very active and more than vigilant in their vocation. It was 10 o'clock before we all left the ferry landing. We laid too the balance of the day on this beautiful spot. The sick are not mending.

9th July. We rolled together this morning breaking up our corrals and stringing in order on the road. We moved about 13 miles and tolerable water and grass on a small creek where the hills, mountains and red buttes make a picturesque appearance. I am this day in bad health but after drinking a cup of tea for supper I feel much better. It is the first cold I have taken on the travel. The sick are still mending.

10th July. Traveled 15 miles over a good road for a mountainous country. We passed the Willow Spring and believe it is good water as I have seen on the road. Last night there was fears entertained that our cattle would be poisoned by drinking the water, but none of them died up to this time. Encamped there we had good water and grass.

11th July. Traveled 16 miles and reached that noted encampment at Independence Rock. This rock is a great curiousity.

It is near one mile in circumference and 150 feet high at the highest point, you can ascend the rock easy. It lay on Sweet Water River about 165 miles from Laramie. There are hundreds of names inscribed on this rock, it having a tolerable smooth surface giving facilities for inscribing thereon. This rock got its camp by a celebration of the 4th of July by some emigrants to the jumping off west.

12th July. Traveled 10 miles. This evening I made a tour of some 3 miles to a neighboring mountain. Two other journeyed with me. We ascended the mountain side some 2000 feet and lacked a hundred feet of reaching the top. We sat down among the rocks, for these mountains are nothing but rocks with now and then a cedar or pine, and consulted whether we should descend or ascend, finally concluded to descend. Had not proceeded far when we discovered a flock of mountain sheep. Mr. Bennett (one of the company) fired upon them and badly wounded one, but night prevented our succeeding in getting our mutten. We enjoyed our ramble very much. The scenery bold and romantic. The rocks are composed of lava*. Springs are common in those stupendous piles of rock. The deep chasms, fissures and obstructions makes it very dangerous to stroll in the —— of nature hiding places so I am satisfied with the ramble and shall not take another until I reach the place of destination.

This morning (it was cloudy) the clouds below the peak of a mountain for the first time in my life. We had a very pleasant encampment, all cheerful and gay. The mountains rising in majestic grandeur on both sides, the beautiful little Sweet Water, so clear and limpid is its water and so are all of the creeks putting into it, with their gravelly beds and sandy bottoms.

13th July. Traveled 16 miles, over a sandy plain, still up Sweet

Water. This is the only pass to the great south pass. A few more days will bring us to the point when we will have to say we are out of the Mississippi Valley.

14th July. Moved 15 miles over a good road for a mountain pass crossing Sweet Water several times. One of my wagoners shot a buffalo with others. The buffalo have ran into the train. We are well supplied with fresh meat. I was on a little hunting excursion when all this happened,* the buffalo threw the women into dismay. Artemisia to wild sage has been all the firewood for several days. It grows more luxuriant here than at any other place I have seen, growing 8 feet high some instances. The sick are mending and will soon be well. Today we saw dead oxen on the road which had died from other trains. We had a small quantity of rain for four days in succession, although this portion of the country has the reputation of being dry. The dust is very bad most of the road.

15th July. Traveled 18 miles and encamped on Sweet Water. Capt. Childs lost a very valuable steer today. The road still good. We passed some saleratus lakes, but they were not so large as some we have passed heretofore. It can be gathered in great abundance. It forms an incrustation on the ground. Sometimes as much as 6 or 8 inches thick, a most beautiful article, as transparent as glass though I am of the opinion that the most transparent is not the best. We also had a most cheerful hailstorm. It pelted the poor wagoners, while the aristocracy of the company were secure from the storm. This morning I had a chill, the effects of cold, and saw at a great distance the Wind River mountains practically covered with snow.

16th July. Moved forward 16 miles, fine grass and the best of water. The fact is the story told by those displeased Oregonites is all a hoax. The grass is very good except a few places on the north fork of the Platte.

We traveled very fast today it being cool and cloudy and some rain fell in the afternoon. We rose two hills putting us upward more than 2000 feet. They were quick in succession of each other. There was to be a fine view of the Wind River Mountains again. They rose in towering heights above us. The snow was plainly visible in their deep cuts and chasms near their summits. Encamped in a beautiful little hollow here. I drank the best water I have ever drank, clear of all mineral influences which is uncommon on the Platte and its tributaries.

17th July. Traveled 14 miles over a good road to be so near those perpetual snowy mountains. Yesterday there was some discontent in the train in consequence of uproarious gentlemen taking the lead before turn. Today all are in their places and quietude prevails. Orders disobeyed are always attended with bad effects. Encamped on Sweet Water for the last time. The great south pass we shall see tomorroiw and I will give you what I can see of it.

18th July 1848. Beautiful morning, clear, calm, and cool. Geared up and made for the Pacific Spring. In making the travel we passed the South Pass. This is one of the most noted points on the route. This pass divided the water of the Mississippi and those winding their way to the Pacific. For the last three or 4 miles the road leading to this pass does not ascend more than 5 feet to the hundred. On the right as you approach the pass the low hills come within a few hundred yards of the road. The same may be said of the left until you pass the culmination point when they raise quite abruptly and to considerable height. After passing through we ran down a small hollow some two miles to the Pacific Spring. Wagons making it without locking or any difficulty in holding back. Just suppose thousands of wagons and teams crossing the great ridge dividing the waters of the Atlantic and Pacific without an effort, at the height of near 8000 feet above the Gulf of Mexico and that too in the immediate vicinity and in full view of the snow capped mountains and you will come to the conclusion that this pass was washed out by nature's hand for great and noble purposes in days and years yet to roll by.

I will now make a few remarks upon the face of the country through which we have passed, from what is called the boundary line between the State of Missouri and the Indian Territory to the crossing of the south fork of the Platte. The soil is generally good with a fine award of grass. From that point to the south pass is generally dry, sandy and without timber, except willows now and then a few short and very indifferent cottonwood. The mountains are timbered with the different kinds of pine and cedar though the greater portion of them are composed of rock, none of them having snow on their summit but the Wind River Mountains and only seeing the southern portion of them the snow could only be seen in the deep ravines* where the sun had but little influence. Traveled 10 miles.

19th July. Traveled 20 miles over a good road and encamped on Little Sandy where we enjoyed a good night's rest. Those sick a few days ago are well but still there is some sickness in camp though not of a serious character. The nights are cool and the days quite warm. Left camp and drove five miles and encamped on Big Sandy Creek where we shall remain tomorrow, having before us a dry trail of 40 miles which must be made during the evening and morning. We passed the balance of the day in camp. Some are washing, some trading and still a portion hunting. I find men in these mountains that have been here 25 years. A Mr. Kincaid is now in camp trading with our men, he having some 200 head of cattle which we need in some measure. This gentleman (Kincaid) removed to these mountains from Boone County, Missouri in the year 1824. He is quite an old man, yet active, although he has been injured in the leg as he is lame. Persons of a weakly constitution should visit these mountains and remain one winter in them and if he has the fire of life in him sufficient to bear a year* he will get to be a stout man. If he should not have that fire of life in him, he will fall a victim to his complaint. We see a great many graves on the way, but when we consider the number of sickly habits we should not be surprised. Those men living here have generally taken squaws and have large families. They are very profligate and pay a high price to the emigrants for all they buy. Powder $1, sugar 50¢, domestic cotton 40¢, coffee 40¢, bacon 10¢, flour 12¢ per lb. When you buy of them the following prices may be taken. As common for a buffalo well dressed $3, $1 mockasins per pair, 50¢ to $1, dressed skins doe $1, elk $2. These prices vary according to the size of the skin. This evening closes the day with all the beauties of a clear and calm evening in the mountains (21st July). This morning quite as calm as the evening preceding. The mountaineers still trading. Capt. Childs informs me he will leave this evening at 4 o'clock and then for a long drive in the night. I will give you the particulars when the drive is over. At 3 o'clock we struck out for Green River. When we had traveled 1½ miles from Big Sandy we passed a small butte 45 feet high and having no name. We gave it the name of Smith's Butte in honor of a Mr. Smith who is a fellow wagoner in the train. We drove on until night called a halt and boiled the tea kettle, supped and then drove all night at sunrise the 22nd halted for breakfast, after which we moved forward and reached Green River at 3 o'clock. Our cattle very much fatigued and ourselves not very well rested after a sleepless night, having traveled 40 miles in 24 hours. In making down the bluff or mountain I should call it, we found it very steep, in fact we traveled over a very rough road the latter part of the stretch.

23rd July. We lay by today and I have an opportunity of seeing up and down the river and to the buttes on either side which is quite a short view. The buttes on the river are very high and of a greying white sometimes inclined to blue and red. The bottoms are low with lakes and some incrustations of salt. The water in the river good and clear; the current quick at the rate of 6 miles per hour. On some islands in the river there is a beautiful grove of cottonwoods. Timber being very rare in this country, I feel like calling any place beautiful that grows a few trees if they could be indifferent. Nature certainly has made a wonderful display of the mountains making principal, differing very much from the timbered mountains on the head of the Ohio. There timber and woodland cap the heights while in the Rocky Mountain scarcely a tree of any height is to be found. Artemisia is the only shrub of any note. It grows all over the whole country even in the tops of the mountains. We lost two oxen out of the train by death last night. They generally look well. There are some mountaineers here trading with our people, dressed skins, shirts and pantaloons are all the go here. We shall see many traders in this portion of the country. The Snake tribe holds here. I have been two months in the train traveling to the far west and I must say a more heavy business I never performed. Traveling with a family cross this American desert is the very hardest business I have ever followed. I was very near forgetting to state that Green River is about 120 yards wide and runs to the left, winding its way to the Gulf of California.

The weather has been fine, quite cool at night and warm during the day. It has been smoky for several days preventing view at a distance.

27

24th July 1848. At 9 o'clock this morning we struck tent and ran down the river about 1½ miles and there came to a butte or bluff so very steep as to require two teams to one wagon (this is what we call doubling). We then made it very easy. Then in about two miles further we reached a hollow or deep gorge in the mountain, ran up it some distance and then passed on top the mountain again and ran back parallel with the road in the hollow, then returning to the right when we made another hollow that led us to the* fork of Green River ran up it so as to make 8 miles and encamped on the best grass I have seen for many days. On this stream we passed a spring, the best or as good as any I ever drank of, the water being so cold that it made my teeth ache. I must here record a fact worthy of note. I weighed 245 lbs when I left the states. I was weighed a few days ago and I only drew 194 lbs so here is a falling off of 49 lbs and more health and* strength and action enjoyed than when at the greatest weight. I attribute this falling off to the manner of life rather* than anything else. The want of vegetable and proper seasoning contributes very much to reduce me, being of a billious temperment when fed upon luxuries, has caused a decline of flesh in this abstimous mode of living.

25th July. We traveled 10 miles today over hill and dale and encamped at or near a spring below which there is quite a grove of fir wood. It is quite tall and as much as 3 feet over two feet from the ground, tapering in the most regular order with limbs springing from the trunk from the ground to the top. Inter-mixed with this growth is the small sour cottonwood whose leaves are said to be poisonous. It does not grow large at any rate. I have not seen any more than 6 inches in diameter and say 25 feet high. I took a short hunt this morning. Saw plenty of game, say about 40 antelope, but was unsuccessful in killing any. At a late hour I strode into camp having walked some 7 or 8 miles with my rifle and game taking accoutrements, a journey I could not have performed in 2 days one year ago. This is the effect a mountain life has upon those who are bloated up with disease. I would advise all those who are slightly troubled with dispepsia to take a mountain trip. It is almost sure to cure them. It is quite cool and I look for frost tonight. We are immediately under some tall hills. The wind continued. No frost but there was ice in camp ½ inch thick.

26th July. Left camp earlier than common and traveled 18 miles. At our noon halt Joseph Walker, the noted mountaineer met us. He is a very fine looking man. The very picture of health and discourses well on most topics. He continued with the train through the evening. He conducted us through a pass in these mountains by which means we avoided a very steep hill both up and down. Mr. Walker appears to be about 45 years of age and steps with the elasticity of a youth but this much may be said of any one that has lived in these mountains a few years. To see life the boyancy of a mountaineer compared to one of Missouri's sons would astonish the most of men. There is quite a number of men from the states throughout this mountain wilderness. They tell us there is more real pleasure in one year in the mountains than a whole lifetime in a dense settled country. There is no political pursuits to tire and weary the limbs and last but not least no law or lawyers to pettifog among them to mar their peace and sow discord among them. Their duties are confined to the horse and gun and when they become tired of one place they remove to another. Their squaws performing all the labor. We are encamped on a fork of Green River.

We lay by today. The women are washing and cooking which things are indespensable. The men are trading, the mountain boys having followed us from Green River, buying and selling horses, skins, mockasins, whip thongs, etc. The little girls are merily playing around the camp while the little boys are as much delighted with their fishing and bringing willows to make fire. This morning we had quite a frost though the day is warm for all practicle purposes. The grass is very good. Ham's Fork is about 20 yards wide with plenty of water to run any quantity of machinery. The quaking asp shows in all the hills though it is of a dwarfish growth.

Our encampment shows quite a stir. This evening some five or 8 mountain men are here drinking alcohol at $1 a pint and they are very mellow. They have rare sport.

28th July. Traveled 11 miles over a very rough road. We climbed* a* hill some 2000 feet above our encampment and continued on high ground until noon when we rested our teams a few minutes on the most lively spot I have seen since I left the States. Flora had covered the mountain tops with her many colored dress and among the variety was seen the blue phlox in full bloom. To the left still higher on the mountain was a beautiful grove of fir encircled with quaking asp. On the right hand was a grove of asp alone. Near 1½ miles from our nooning we passed through a mixed grove of asp and fir and continued upward to the top of a mountain, then down the mountain and it was certainly a long trip not less than 1½ miles and in one place we had to let our wagons down by ropes not depending on the team. We are now encamped in a very romantic spot enclosed by mountains on every side, a small branch leading out. The very best of water and tolerable good grass.

One of the families migrating with us left the train for the Salt Lake Valley. We are traveling a cutoff which leaves Fort Bridger about 40 miles to the south having left the route traveled by Fremont. Frost has been seen for four mornings in succession.

28th July. Traveled 20 miles over quite a rough country

indeed, up one mountain and down another.

Today we reached Bear River. It is a beautiful stream about 80 yards wide, the current not more than 3 miles to the hour. We do not cross this stream, but travel some 4 or 5 days down it. This beautiful stream runs into the noted Salt Lake in the valley of which the Mormons have located as a retreat from all civilization. At our encampment this evening we have a Mr. Smith who has been so unfortunate as to lose one of his legs. He is a fine looking mountaineer. Good grass and plenty of river water.

30th July 1848. Moved forward so as to make 13 miles over some rough ground encamped on a small branch in the mountains. I see where the road takes the mountain. The reason of the mountain encampment is in consequence of the river sweeping immediately under the foot of the mountain. We leave this river on our left hand. Its run this far has been very much to the north but it certainly must soon make a turn to the south because the Salt Lake is south of us. These are called the blue mountains, the name not being very appropriate. They have a light coat of vegetation on them, but almost bare of what is called timber.

31st July. Rolled out this morning and pulled up the steepest and longest hill we have met with one mile farther on and down on and on to Bear River, having been pushed out from it by the mountains. Made 8 miles and encamped on the bank of B. River. Fine grass and river water. Snow in sight, supposed to be 25 miles off. I caught a salmon trout today so you see I have been fishing in this wilderness of mountains. The health of the camp is now very good. Although all in camp are never well at the same time. We have been very fortunate to lose none by casualty or death.

1 August 1848. The train took the trail* this morning and moved off in good stile and made 20 miles over good road, crossing

several small streams running into Bear River. I will here attempt to describe one of them where we nooned. The brook (for it could be called nothing else) ran across the bottom at right angles or nearly so with a strong current hurrying on as though it was to offer some facilities to civilization. In fact I looked down it if I could not see the place of usefulness, but no the limpid stream was hurrying to mingle its waters with those of a hundred kind and to make up the stream of streams that empty into the Salt Lake which has no connection with any sea or ocean, having a system of waters entirely of its own. Camped in a canyon where we had plenty of wood, water and grass. The true Oregon grass here makes its appearance.

August 2nd. We struck tent and moved forward over some rough ground on Bear River the lowland of which are good in most places. The purest little streams issuing from the mountains crossing the bottom at 3 or 4 miles distant from each other. Just suitable for irrigating the arible parts of it. Traveled 18 miles on the 2nd of August.

Late in the evening we encamped at the noted encampment of the Soda Springs. I have taken some pains to see something at this place. There is a number of springs that are strongly impregnated with the carbon of iron, some of them as clear and limpid as the purest oil while others are quite the contrary being the color of beer. The waters have a wholesome* influence on the system when drank of. These springs are situated on Bear River about 60 miles east of Fort Hall and near 1300 from Independence, Missouri. The Steamboat Spring which is the same class of water is about 300 yards from the present road to the left hand requires a special remark. It issues from a hole in a rock about 6 inches in diameter which rock has been formed by the incrustation of the evaporation of the water. This rock rises about 6 feet above the water in the Bear

River and not more than 12 feet distant. It is what might be called a warm spring flowing about 10 gallons per minute. It boils and obulates and even throws 2½ and 3 feet high by a current of gas, strongly impregnated as before noted. I laid off my hat and adjusted my clothing so as to bathe my face thinking that if it had a wholesome influence on the system when drank it would have a like influence when bathed in. Nature has dealt out bountifully of her best gifts here. She has given the life invigorating stream, a beautiful little river, a mountainous and healthy country, also a tolerable good soil and mountain streams to irrigate it, fine and wholesome grass for any quantity of cattle. The very ground on which these springs are situated are nicely decorated with the evergreens of the forest. Add to all this the magnificent grandeur of the surrounding mountains covered with pine cedar, fir and quaking asp. Here everything does allure and must time attract the capitalist and fashionable as well as the valetudinarians of the land.

About midway between the upper spring and the Steamboat Spring there is a mill site where the water could be thrown upon an overshot wheel 22 feet in diameter. This little stream runs under a natural bridge which the road crosses and falls into Bear River.

The water taken from these springs is much better than saleratus to mix up bread stuff. It rises very well and is much sweeter. We lay by today for the purpose of exploring and taking some recreation at this place of all places seen on this trip.

I took a stroll late in the evening towards the foot of a mountain and northern direction from the encampment and near the mountain there was a small lake 300 yds long by near 30 yds in breadth strongly impregnated with the same gas as those on the river. Following the lake quite to the mountain I came to a spring of the best soda water that I have seen during the day and you may rely I saw and tested all that came in my way. One of our young men killed a badger or some kind of animal not common only in those mountains. It was 18 inches high and about 3 feet long, having very long claws on the forefeet, with a white strip beginning on the head and extending beyond the shoulders.

4th August. Geared up and rolled out down Bear River some 6 miles where we left it, turned the spur of a mountain and came to another soda spring, not of equal celebrity of those we had left, but very good. Traveled 18 miles today. Capt. Childs wagon broke down. One of the wheels falling into picas a printer would say. The tire broke in two places, 4 spokes and two fellies out of the rim. Hallo here come the wagon into camp. The captain has taken a cold meld and the tire and all is made good. The country over which we passed today carries marks of volcanic action. The rocks having the appearance of being burnt and by examination I found them to be very hard and porous. I should not be astonished if in a few years these rocks or similar ones should be used for mill stones instead of sending to France for them. They are hard, sharp and porous, three of the principal qualities of the French Stone. They appear only in color (which is not essential) being of bluish cast. Our encampment for the first time is on the waters of Lewis River, the principal stream of the Columbia. The little stream close by is called the Portneuff.

5th August. Traveled 18 miles over a good road. It appears to be a basin in the mountains. The volcanic appearance not so evident today. Encamped at the head of a willow thicket on the small branch. A very warm and calm evening, but very smoky having the likeness of Indian Summer. It will be cold before morning. Below zero no doubt.

6th August. Moved forward 16 miles traveling by cannons (sic) through the mountains. I will here give a description of a cannon. It is nothing more than a hollow closely shut in by mountains and where two heads together and run a different direction. It makes a low pass in the hill or mountain and very often a good road can be had, so as to save ground and heavy pulling. A part of the road today very rough.

7th August. Remained in camp all day. I visited the fort. I found Capt. Grant (who is a proprietor) quite communicative. Mrs. Stewart and May visited in company with me. We had a social conversation with Mrs. Maxwell (whose husband was absent on business to Ft. Vancouver). We found this lady to be intelligent and quite accomplished.

This fort is situated on Snake or Lewis River in latitude 45-25 north. Everything appears in order, and carried out according to rule. It is about 80 feet square, the rooms placed inside the outer walls, some of them two stories high. I saw nothing of a warlike character except a rifle or two which are very useful articles in a country like this. Snake River is near 140 yards wide with a smooth gentle current not exceeding 3 miles per hour. The traders follow the train as though their salvation depended on the trade with them. There is at this time not less than a dozen of them around camp and some of them quite rude in their manners. At this for everything can be had lower than any other point on the road. Horses can be obtained for $25 and good ones at that, but poor* horses are much cheaper in California, therefore the emigrants going through should not buy even here.

9th August. Traveled 12 miles. The train passed the fort and ran down a beautiful plain, crossing several sloughs about 8 miles below the fort, we came to Portneuff again. Here it is quite a river being 800 yds wide, clear and beautiful mountain stream. We are in sight of Snake River. The plain is several miles wide and fine trees along the banks show the line of the river which is very near east and west at this point.

10th August. Traveled 15 miles down Snake or Lewis River. We nooned today one mile above the American Falls. I rode down and took a good look at them. I had been told the fall of water was about 14 feet, but I venture the ascertion, to measure from the bason below to a level of the water above it is not less than 24 feet. These falls from every appearance around the place has in times washed away the rock for near 150 yds and consequently keep getting higher up the river. Most of the water passes the north shore where it pitches and foams and looks as white as snow. Near the middle of the stream is an island almost entirely a map of bare* rock with two or three scrubby cedar. The river at this place is about 250 yds wide. 90 yds will take in all the fall or nearly so. The water is at a low stage and there is sufficient to run a quantity of machinery. The misfortune is there is not soil to support a population. No timber near for firewood. The sage brush grows luxuriantly and that tells the story for it only grows in a light sandy, dry soil. The lowlands are generally very well set with grass, and the highlands with sage to the exclusion of everything else.

I shall hereafter call this Lewis River as all the people of the state should do. The Hudson Bay Company so far as I heard them speak of names studiously avoids all American names. We passed two other places in the river where the fall of water was considerable, one about 4 feet, the other near ten feet in a few yards. The last named place might be called Rapids with propriety, poor grass and branch water ½ mile from the river.

Struck tent and rolled on down the river. The bluffs present a perpendicular appearance. Lewis River has become quite a rapid stream being near 600 yards wide, fall succeeding fall which would prevent navigation if called for. The scenery rich, the mountains seen at a distance, the plains very much cut up with depressions which enable me to say we had a bad road and clouds of dust to contend with. We crossed fall creek. It has old beaver dam after dam and the water pouring over them keeps a continual roaring as though a storm was at hand. Traveled 13 miles then encamped on the river. Grass not abundant.

We ran down a short hill today and crossed a small branch to look upon you would suppose was not practicable.

12th August. Traveled 10 miles over a tolerable road for the country. We passed the Oregon road today and encamped on Raft Creek at an early hour. All appears to be cheerful and hiliarity. We are on the way to California for certain.

Sunday 13th August. Traveled 25 miles over quite smooth road on Cajeux or Raft Creek. One ox died and two gave out, but got them in camp. The plain on this creek is large for the size of the stream. In crossing it today the tongue of a wagon was broke entirely out. Then with 3 log chains we made a tongue and ——and done 10 miles. The grass is good with tolerable branch water. I will here remark that branch water in those mountains is as good or better than the water used in Missouri, especially the sistern water so much used in the lower part of that state.

Monday 14th. We only moved 3 miles today, almost always after a hard day's drive we lay by in order to rest our cattle. The last 700 miles of the road has been to all appearances much worse on cattle than the forepart of the journey withstanding the teams are much better off than when we were at Fort Laramie. There are but few that know the worth of oxen in the states. I am confident if a team of cattle was taken and treated with humanity that they would travel across the continent at the rate of 400 miles a month, but the inhuman treatment of drivers is enough to destroy a number of teams. Men are by ox driving like they are by everything else, some not fit to carry a whip within a mile of a team. Driving is reducing to system and he that drives to let others know he is driving will soon have no team to drive. The fact is every attention to your cattle is actually necessary to take you through this trip. Oxen are the central object on this route and you belong to them instead of them to you.

This evening we made tongue and —— for the broken wagon in short order and it performs well.

Tuesday 15th August, 1848, traveled 13 miles, good roads up Cajuix Creek. The scenery bold and rich, peak after peak riding to great height on both sides of our road. The plain on the creek quite narrow but makes a fine mountain pass. Encamped on another branch of the creek. A few of the Digger tribe of Indians in camp selling berries. The mountain black* berry is certainly the most delicious of any I ever tasted. They are black when ripe.

Wednesday 16th August. Traveled 16 miles and encamped in a basin of the mountains. Here all the language I command will not describe the scenery around our encampment. It is rich beyond anything I have ever beheld. Single and isolated rocks standing on the plain from 50 to 200 feet high, encircled by a chain just giving admission and dismission to and from the basin. We passed over the roughest piece of road today that has been seen on the journey. Large rocks lying partly under the ground with their edges turned all directions so as to make it very rough. One of the wagons parted coupling pole. If a mountain destroying angel has been dispatched here with power to disclose and scatter the elements of mountains, he could not have done more than has been done here. Rugged peaks, projecting rocks, deep canyons and gorges are all here. I took a mountain stroll today and saw a few of the curiosities to be found in those stupendous mountains. I am sorry that I have no leisure to take long and frequent tramps in those places frequented only by the breath of the forest. My mind is ever active, my eyes always open to see those towering heights. The mountains have been continually in view for the last 700 miles. As fast as one chain would be lost in the distance another would come into view not withstanding the weather has been smoky all the time.

Thursday 17th Aug. Started early and traveled 20 miles over a very rough road. Several steep hills to go down. Had to lock 2 wheels 4 times during the day. We are encamped on Goose Creek, which makes its way in Lewis River. On yesterday we was (sic) on the waters running into the Salt Lake.

Major Hensley who left us at Independence Rock with the mule train overtook us today. He intended to pass to Fort Bridger and thence south to Salt Lake intending to follow ——— trail. He passed on without difficulty until he reached the southwestern portion of the Lake and traveled several miles upon an incrustation of salt and unfortunately for the Major and his train, (ten in number) there fell a heavy rain which so weakened the incrustation that they were very near perishing in the mire. They were under the necessity of cutting loose the packs to save the animals, in this way they lost their provisions or nearly so with part of their clothing. They were 48 hours without food and water and hard at work most of the time to save the property. They then retraced their steps to the Mormon City and there replenished their larder. They had been absent from us 36 days. I was glad to see the train but felt fearful something had happened knowing there was good mountaineers and energetic men in that little band.

Friday 18th. Traveled 16 miles up Goose Creek today. We passed a warm spring, too warm for comfort. The country through which we have passed today has once been in a high state of volcanic action judging from every appearance. Willows for firewood and branch water to drink and when we have better I will tell it.

Saturday August 19th. Traveled 18 miles, the greater portion of which was good. We left Goose Creek and are now on waters unknown by anyone in camp, although it is believed they run into Salt Lake.

We are on high ground and consequently the mountains appear low. I will remark here that there is a great difference between what is called Artemisia and sage. The Artemisia has little or no smell when bruised while when the sage is bruised the odor is very offensive. The latter grows in abundance on our line of travel.

Sunday 20th Aug. Traveled 20 miles, made a late start and encamped at 10 o'clock at night. All the camp were very much displeased at the unusual and unnecessary drive during the night. The dust being so very bad and with the darkness of the night made it dangerous in the extreme to the families who had to go in wagons. The present encampment is without wood and water not abundant. Sage brush ½ mile off which is the poorest wood known, Buffalo chips not excepted.

We believe ourselves to be in California south of the parallel of 42 North. The Digger Tribe of Indians are our neighbors for 300 miles and have been for the last 100. They speak the Snake language and are of the same family though distinct in territory. Their territory being in a manner destitute of game they are very poor, almost entirely naked and with all very filthy, living principally upon roots and small insects such as crickets, ants, etc.

Monday 21st August. Traveled 8 miles and corralled for the day. The road ran along a plain at the upper end of which we found the hot springs, strongly impregnated with sulphur. In looking around the spring I picked out a hole near the large body of water about 2 ounces of sulphur as pure as that purchased at the shops. In taste, smell and by calcimining it proved to be quite pure, but a short distance from the springs runs as pure a little stream of good water as ever I drank of. This is certainly a wonderful country. Wonderful rivers to be a source of benefit to the unborn millions that are to be reared in the great Mississippi Valley. The greatest valley on the globe while the mountains will give us furs and minerals* for ages to come. 5 o'clock, I have just returned from the hot springs and while there I shaved, a great luxury sure. These springs are spread over an area of an acre. The ground is quite warm. This is another great watering place or is to be in time.

Tuesday 22nd. Traveled 13 miles, good road, water and grass, wood scarce. There is in the vicinity of this camp various pools some of them deep enough to swim in. I saw a yearling pulled out of one and might have drowned if it had remained in the water. This is the first encampment on the waters of Mary River. The springs at this place are worthy of notice. The ground around them is raised from one half to 3 feet and there appears to be a fountain that would supply even a city. You may stand 15 or 20 feet from the center of the low mound (where the water is seen) and by stamping your feet put the water in motion. It appears to be entirely hollow. The turfs of grass are very strong bearing a wagon and team.

Wednesday 23rd Aug. Traveled 8 miles and passed through a canyon that shall be called the Vale of Horrors. Of all the places that I ever saw a wagon go over, a part of this canyon is with worst, jumping rocks that actually looks unreasonable for a four wheeled carriage to pass, although 32 wagons and 2 carriages passed with entire safety. We are now encamped on the branch of Mary River in a beautiful plain where the grass is abundant. We are taking all possible care of our teams because everything depends on them. Major Hensley left our camp very early this morning with the mule train. It is expected that Mr. ——— will return to us in the California mountains with supplies, not that we expect to want them but to be sure not to be in danger of suffering.

This is a very interesting part of the journey. The many warm springs, the snow capped mountains and the beautiful plains very agreeably decorated with flowers all go to interest the weary wagoner on this tour through the dust that is almost enough to suffocate. A very pleasant evening, quite cool.

Thursday 24th. Traveled down Mary's River 17 miles. A rich and beautiful plain the whole distance. The stream is quite small, the water does not cascade*. Encampments are to be had at any given point. The grass good but dry for the season. This is our 3rd camp on this stream. We expect to travel slow in order to keep our teams in good order for the mountains. We are getting more watchful knowing this to be the most dangerous river that we have passed. To the left is a tall range of mountains which marks the line of this little river.

Friday 25th Aug. Traveled 15 miles and made our fourth encampment on the Creek of Mary's River. The best grass that I have seen for many days. The lowland is from 1 to 2 miles wide, very rich and produces a heavy coat of vegetation. We met a train of packs from California, 23 in number. Several of them had specimens of gold lately discovered in that country about 70 miles above Sutters establishment. They represented the mines as being very rich yielding on an average of two ozs. of gold to the days labor and that one particular man had made 700 dollars in a day. The train giving this information were Mormons bound for the Salt

Lake Valley.

Saturday 26th. Traveled 17 miles, 5th camp on this stream. We cross 3 low hills the river running through as many canyons. In the afternoon we ran down a beautiful plain near 8 miles. The mountains quite bold on the left while they appeared at a distance on the right. The Digger Indians made their appearance but they kept out of camp. A strict guard is around the cattle.

A gentleman named Antwine who joined our train on packhorse on Bear River, had 3 horses stolen from him 2 days ago and he has returned to camp this evening without them.

The Digger Indians of all that we have passed through, are the most dangerous. They sulk about the watering places and shoot the stock with their bows and arrows.

It was in this nation that Comodore Stockton was wounded last fall while in camp. It would be very pleasant to see timber for I do not know how long it has been since I saw anything that could be called a tree. Not since we left Lewis River. Fine grass, had water, willows for firewood.

Sunday 27th August. Traveled 10 miles down Mary River. We are just at the head of a canyon through which the river runs. We shall take the hills for our road. The plain continued thus far, also the mountains on the left or southeast of the river. Some of the Digger Family are in camp, almost naked. In fact a man grown has to make use of a small piece of skin as a fig leaf or he would be in the state he was born.

Our stock is guarded day and night and will be until we reach the heights of the California Mountains which are called Sierra Nevada Mountains.

Monday 28th. Traveled 16 miles until noon we ran down a canyon crossing the river frequently. The afternoon the road kept the plain. This canyon is rather singular in many places. The rocks are perpendicular while in others it slopes back so as to admit a road. (Canion is a Spanish term and has the same meaning that the term canyon means in English.) When in a canion properly speaking you must go forward until you get out. If you can get on the plain to the right or left even with difficulty it would be called a gorge or hollow. The scenery was rich, touching the sublime.

Tuesday 29th Aug. Traveled 23 miles through clouds of dust and part of the time rough road. At our encampment we met 17 wagons from California. They had near 100 head of horses and some cattle bound for the Salt Lake being a part of Cooks Battalion. They were returning from the services of their country and had with them a small piece of ordinance (sic). I did not inquire but expected it was a trophy they were carrying along won by their arms. The landscape was most beautiful, one mountain upon another in amphitheatre style. The valley very level with some sloughs. No wood convenient not even sage brush but willows at a distance and river water. Upon the whole it was a poor camp had not even grass sufficient.

Wednesday 30th. We ran 13 miles. Fine camp. Plenty of dry willows and grass, even water, but the glowing stories of the Mormons of the gold mines nearly ran us all mad.

Thursday 31st Aug. Traveled 14 miles and made our tenth camp on Mary's River, grass good, large willows for wood. The mountains are of medium height on both sides of the plain. No timber to be seen nor a shrub of any kind save the willows which line the river in abundance. The mountains appear entirely bare and present a smooth appearance.

On this river (very small to have the name river) we anticipated a great deal of sickness. The camp notwithstanding is in better health at any period since we left the States. Health prevails throughout the camp.

Friday, 1st September 1848. Traveled 15 miles and our eleventh camp on Mary's River. The dust has been intolerable bad, rising in clouds from the train as it moved down the plain. A part of the road today was covered with dust so strongly impregnated with saleratus that it caused every living thing to sneeze that inhaled it. If we had been traveling through lime to the same depth it would not have been more disagreeable. The landscape still beautiful, the day very cool with flying clouds and heavy squalls of wind from the northwest.

Saturday 2nd Sept. Traveled 18 miles and pitched out twelfth camp on this river. The plain was covered with a saline incrustation. The day was very cold and cloudy. The clouds appeared to hang on the mountain tops. It rained on the plain this evening and snowed on the mountains. The tops of them looking as white as silver.

Sunday Sept. 3rd. Traveled 9 miles down a beautiful plain and encamped the 13th time on Mary's River. The mountains are bold and above the medium height. The plain which Mary's River runs through must be near 5000 feet above the Gulf of Mexico. Still there are mountains rising to the same height above the plains which we are in. We must be near the parallel of 41 North. I omitted mentioning James Davidson who was teamster of Mr. Smith was very much injured by the bursting of a shot gun, mutilating his face and right hand. None of the wounds appear dangerous. This accident happened Friday night while on guard.

Monday 4th Sept. Traveled 13 miles and pitched our 14th camp on this river. The road very good, grass good. Last night and also tonight the mountains bold and rugged. The plain very narrow but at this place quite extensive. The day is very warm. I find the weather changeable here as elsewhere. Frost has been of common occurrence for the last 400 or 500 miles. There is a plant that grows in abundance on this little river which is very salty and for want of a better name I shall call it Saline Plant. The Indians make great use of it either as salt or for food. I have seen large quantities of it collected and laying in the plain. I do not recollect of any one ever saying anything about this plant although it certainly deserves the notice of those acquainted with botany.

Tuesday 5th Sept. Traveled 15 miles and pitched our 15th camp on this little river. The scenery continues near the same as heretofore. The day very warm, grass good, wood difficult to get at having to cross the river and float it over. At this camp we found a mule belonging to Hensley's Train pierced with arrows so as to prevent it from traveling. It becomes my duty to record an accident which happened this evening while on guard. A pistol in the hands of Mr. Misner unfortunately went off and entered the fleshy part of the arm above midway from the shoulder of Mr. Smith to the elbow. There is some censure attached to the unfortunate Misner but taking all the circumstances together I see no reason for censure whatever. The whole camp sympathizes with Mr. Smith and it was certainly a serious affair. His teamster being badly mutilated by the bursting of a shot gun a few days ago leaving him in a rather helpless condition.

Mr. Misner who is quite a discreet young man and in bad health is as much cut down from the accident as anyone can be.

Wednesday 5th Sept. Traveled 20 miles and made our 16th camp on this river. Nothing of interest to note. Good grass and willows plenty.

I haven't seen a tree yet (that is from Lewis River here).

Thursday 7th Sept. Traveled 20 miles and pitched 17th camp

46

on this little stream. Willows scarce and grass not very plenty. The last two days has been quite warm about summers heat. The nights are cool. The mountains rugged and picturesque. An incrustation of saline efflorescence covers the plain almost entirely for the last three days.

Friday 8th. Traveled 4 miles and encamped on the river making the 18th time that we have corralled on the stream. A general repairing of wagons with the men, the women are washing. All is good humor and high spirits. The grass good. The mountains bold and rugged. The water bad and we expect it to be no better until this river leaves us as it will do in a few days more.

Saturday 9th Sept. 1848. Traveled 6 miles and encamped the 19th time. We met today another portion of Cooks (it will be remembered they are Mormons) just from California. The glowing gold stories were rehearsed and I have no doubt but what fortunes are realized in a very short time. There were packers.

Sunday 10th. Traveled 15 miles. At 4 o'clock this morning we were aroused from our slumbers and shortly after daylight it was discovered that some of our cattle were pierced with arrows. The cow beasts and one horse were mortally wounded. We detached six men to watch the animals and the train moved forward and in a few minutes after we started the sound of their rifles was heard. They shot an Indian and suppose they killed him. This is the first time we have been molested by Indians. Nothing but diligence will save our stock in guarding them.

Monday 17th Sept. Traveled 16 miles over what may be termed a salaratus plain and made our 20th camp. We met too, another company bound for Salt Lake. The glowing stories about the gold mines in Alta, California. These wagons, 12 in number, came a new route over the mountains and represent it much better than the old road. Our Indian war yesterday has not proved as yet any disadvantage.

Tuesday 12th. We traveled 35 miles during the day and night and made our 21st camp on this stream. It was 4 o'clock in the morning. We were forced into this drive for the want of grass. We had a delightful time driving the teams during the night. The moon fulled at an early hour and shone with great clearness, but all at once she appeared to be covered with clouds, it grew quite dark. I looked and behold the shadows of the earth had fallen on her. The eclipse was total and of course lasted for some time. The Indian fires were plainly to be seen on the right and left. It is their custom when strangers get into their neighborhood to do this in order to give warning to their friends of the fact. Our team gave out but rolled in shortly after daylight. We are now encamped near what is termed the sink of Mary's River and as we have traveled near 300 miles on it, a remark or two would not be amiss. This stream takes its rise within the rim of the great Salt Lake bason. It runs as near as I am able to judge southwest the distance about noted and sinks forming any lake of consequence, except in the snow melting season it may and from every appearance does inundate thousands of acres in and about the sink notwithstanding the banks are very high in that region, say from 20 to 30 feet, the channel narrow never exceeding forty feet. The plain which is extensive, with some very rich spots, but the greater portion is dry and covered with a mixture of salaratus and other substances which are very offensive to those traveling through this country. I feel no hesitation in saying that this whole plain has once been the seat of volcanic action but now, with the exception of a few miles it forms one of the best natural roads that I ever traveled and the only pass known from Fort Hall to upper California. We have dust in quantities on this road which does annoy the members* but proves of great utility to the teams saving their feet from being worn down so they could not make the travel.

Wednesday 13th and night following, at noon today we left the sink of Mary's River where we had poor grass and the worst water we have met with on the road it being very salty and scowering our cattle and several fasted in consequence of that disease. We moved on until 10 o'clock. Stopped without water until 2 o'clock in the morning then run on until the sun had risen we called a halt. You must recollect from the sink we took a new route aiming to strike Salmon Trout River.

Thursday the 14th most of us lay by all the time while others insisted to go forward and the Capt. being ahead of us explored the road. Some 3 wagons got to camp 25 miles from the sink, being out from water or grass 36 hours and our cattle fasting one after another in quick succession and the most of the train being 11 miles from water.

Friday 15th Sept. This day was spent in getting up our fatigued cattle. The most of the teams reached camp on the Salmon Trout River some 10 miles west of a lake of the same name and formed by the river, thus you see this water runs east and is within the great Salt Lake bason. Like many streams in this region they run into lakes and sinks in the spring covering large districts of country but at this season the smaller basons are dry leaving salt plains or marshes.

Sat. 16th. Lay in camp waiting for the wagons and cattle to come in. Reader there are a few trees on the Salmon Trout. Generally cottonwood, some of them 9 feet in circumference. This is the first timber seen since we left Lewis River. The weather is very warm. We have (that is the train) some 25 or 30 head of work cattle. Since we left the sink of Mary's River, the salaratus scowering them and the drive being rather long in such a contingency.

Sunday 17th. All being ready we moved 2 miles and made a new camp where we had grass more abundant. During our stay at the first camp the Indians made beef of several of our work cattle. It is almost impossible to get some men up to their duty.

Monday 18. Left camp early and traveled 5 miles and encamped for the day. Our cattle are in a bad condition and require more nursing. Our course is up this river. Your will perceive that we travel by water courses entirely through this 1500 miles of mountains.

19 and 20 Tuesday and Wednesday traveled 14 miles and continued up Salmon Trout River. The weather very warm, good grass.

Thursday 21st. Traveled 11 miles and encamped on S.T. River. The mountains are bold and rather low to be called mountains. We have intercepted the Mormon's road. We are on our way up the great Sierra Nevada range of mountains. Just after sun down an ox was shot within a few rods* of camp.

Friday 22nd Sept. Struck tent and moved 2 miles and are now at what is called the —— camp. I neglected to mention that on yesterday two of our men returned a few miles for a mare mired. While on the tour they fell in with a party of Diggers and killed 2 of them and came into camp unhurt. A party was detailed to bring in the mare this morning. They fell also in with Diggers and killed one so there has been two Indian battles in as many days. Three killed on one side and on the other not a hair molested.

Traveled 14 miles this morning. We paid our first and last debt of gratitude to a little infant of Mr. Bernett's which was born and lived only a few minutes. It is supposed to be a premature birth. What consolation it should give the parents to be taken by the —— who gave it to enjoy blissful eternity. Their loss is surely its

50

gain.

23, 24, and 25th traveled 40 miles up Salmon Trout. Good road tho dull and uninteresting. We came in view of the timbered mountains. I must say it gave me pleasure to see timber at a distance.

26th Sept. We cut out this morning and ran up to the mouth of a canyon and half the train is now in it. But if it was pleasure to see timber at a distance it must give joy to be in timber, large pine timber. The mountains are very tall and rugged, covered to the summit with a bold little mountain stream running by, the whistling of winds in the trees* all conspire to make one cheerful, but under the circumstances I cannot feel so. We have an awful road before us. Mrs. May is quite sick and unable to do camp duty. Myself just setting up from disease and feel that the hardships before me are more than I should undergo.

27th and 28th Sept. Traveled 5 miles all the way in a canyon and truly it may be called a canyon. The timbered mountains are what I expected in the mountains throughout. The different kinds of pine and cedar and some quaking asp are the only kind of timber found here.

29th. Ran 8 miles above the canyon to what is called Hope or Lake Valley and immediately at the foot of the mountain which will take us one day to make the top. I succeeded in getting one of my wagons on the mountain. I suppose we have not raised less than 3000 feet today. We are now in the snowy region. The mountains there towering above us and snow in every direction in the deep ravines. This is truly a beautiful mountain and different kinds of pine and cedar are the only timber. The rocks are quite picturesque, but the most lovely sight is the beautiful little lakes of fresh water surrounded by meadows* that afford grass in abundance for our many stock.

51

30th Sept. (That day I am 46 years old and on the highest mountain in North America.) This day we succeed in getting all the wagons but 6 on the mountain and ran 3 miles and encamped on one of those beautiful little lakes and I will tell in a day or two when and how we get away from here.

1st. Oct. We lay in camp all day recruiting our teams. We are in what is called Lake Valley. This is quite a pleasant place good water, grass and plenty of wood that makes a blazing fire.

Oct. 2nd. Traveled 4 miles and made the mountain height. We are now near 13,000 feet above the level of the Gulf of Mexico. We also have to run down that height in about 50 miles. Let me tell you I have seen the elephant in the way of mountains. We passed the snow in the mountains and eat of it and it may have fallen there many years ago. The top of the mountain is entirely bare of vegetation. Below the snow the pine grows luxuriantly.

3rd, 4th and 5th Oct. Traveled 30 miles over hill and dale in the Sierra Nevada Mountains and on a new route just opened by the Latter Day Saints. We have experienced a great deal of hardships in getting this far though. The timber of this region is pine and cedar, the undergrowth laurel, ivy and I saw today some oak bushes. It is quite cool, the weather clear. There is a great deal of game in these tallest of mountains.

October 6th. Traveled 15 miles and camped at Sly's Park and it should be called anything else but a park, having no resemblance to any such thing. The timber in this portion of the mountains is delightful. The tall red woods and pine and hemlock with some oak gives the country more beauty than where nothing but bare, arid mountains make their appearance. The birds whistle and sing in every glen and hollow while the evergreen both great and small have an air of cheerfulness that cannot be found only in a timbered country.

7th October. Traveled 8 miles and encamped on a high ridge in the mountains it being the divide between —— and American Rivers. We are several thousand feet lower than when on back bone of this range of mountains, in fact the climate tells me that we are in the neighborhood of being through this highest of mountains in North America. The weather has been very cool for several days in consequence of our great height.

Sunday the 3rd Oct. Traveled 10 miles through the hills and* on the plain bordering on the Sacramento River. The timber is very indifferent, the pine and cedar having given way to oak principally.

9th October. Traveled 4 miles and encamped on a small branch of Weaver's Creek which is noted for its richness of gold mines though not richer than any other little creek in this whole region of country. The gold region is quite extensive 300 miles north and south and varying from 20 to 100 miles in width. Here Weaver Creek near the dry diggins, I unloaded my wagon on the 10th of October and proceeded on to Fort (Sutter) without delay intending to bring back supplies for the winter, being gone two weeks and finding provisions very high I determined to sell my wagon and teams and done so. They brought me 1,100 dollars and in the meantime my health so much endangered that I did not think it advisable to remain in the gold mines. As soon therefore as I could make it convenient I rolled out for the Sacramento River. I remained in the mining district two weeks after my return from the Fort digging a little gold but very feeble indeed being reduced down to 160 pounds or something lower, having lost 86 lbs. of flesh on the travel.

The country from the dry diggins to Sutters Fort for 20 miles is hill and dale, the other is a plain interspersed with oak timber very low and wide spreading tips difficult for wagons to pass under them and thousands of acorns, but no hogs to devour them. Here in the mines salt pork was worth 150 cts. per lbs., beef fresh, from 30 to sixty cents, flour from 50 to 60 cts. per lb., and everything else in proportion. A common calico shirt 8 dollars, shoes from 16 to 20 dollars and so on unto the end of the way of clothing.

We are all having tolerable health. At the end of four weeks we struct (sic) tents and moved onward to the Sacramento passing the fort in the mountains and in 2 miles finding ourselves on the bank of one of the noblest rivers in all alta California, it being near 1000 feet in width here. The tide rises about 3 feet and vessels of a large class can safely arrive.

Here my family and baggage with myself embarked on board a launch which is nothing but the smallest class of sail vessel. We cut out for San Francisco, a considerable town on the south side of a Bay of the same name. We made quite slow progress for 3 or 4 days when we reached the mouth of the river, here we had a fine wind, raised sail and ran through the bay at the rate of 12 miles per hour. Our little bark rode the billows finally and by the by all my family except myself and son William were seasick and heaved all the time. From Sutters landing to this place by water is about 160 miles and land over 200.

So after traveling some 2200 miles by land and water, over hill and mountain and valley, through wet and dry, pleasure and pain and suffering greatly in every way that traveling could bring about we reached this town, San Francisco, on the 11th of November, having been on the way from the States 6 months and four days. And God be thanked our lives were preserved through the whole journey and now find ourselves in better health than when we left the States. Here I close the journal of our travel and hope I shall never see nor undergo the same, although there is much to be learned and to the curious mind, for reflection. And would I think it necessary to say anything more it will be in the form of History of this country so long as I remain in it.

END OF DIARY

* * * * * * * * * * * * * * * * * * * *

I have been in this town, San Francisco, three months and a half and have seen much to amuse and also that would displease the fastidious moralist. We have citizens of the very best moral worth and some that are very disolute-sporting gentlemen of all grades:

Gaming is very common and wine or dram drinking equally as fashionable.

The intelectual worth of the people of this country generally is far ahead of the western states though like all other newly settled places, the inhabitants having very recently passed around the Cape or through the mountains, giving them perhaps the advantage of seeing a great deal more and mixing with the different nations of the earth has put it in their power to become more intelligent on many topics. In religion this country is a low ebb. The Franciscan order of Catholics settled this country some seventy five years ago and having been governed too much by their priests and the priests themselves of very loose habits in morals, it could not be expected that the layity should be a highly refined moral people and again the first emigration of the Anglo Saxon race in order to create friends and find favor among them had to assimilate them in their manners thereby becoming Mexicans by adoption and in this way gaming, dancing and all other amusements which are common in the states is as much practiced on the Sabbath as any other day of the week. The agricultural pursuits of this country are almost destroyed. The quantity of soil considering the extent of territory is quite small although there is some situations highly calculated to produce whatever the husbandman may turn his attention to, the soil being sufficient to produce hemp in some of the valley lands, if I am to judge from the natural growth. I have actually seen the common black mustard which had grown from 8 to 14 feet in height and so thick that it would be impossible to ride through it. But why say anything about agricultural pursuits when the gold is found in such profusion. The ——— improvement of a country cannot progress when the precious metals absorb all other influences. Labor cannot be procured at a fair rate only at seasons when mining cannot be carried on which is winter or rainy seasons.

This country is handsomely situated for commercial purposes. This bay received some noble rivers and is itself one of the best of harbors where vessels of any class can come in with surety of safety. They are arriving daily from the United States laden with provisions and merchandise and also from most of the Pacific Islands as well as from the South American ports. Up to this time there have been but few vessels from China whose rich treasure of notions will shortly find their way into our harbor.

The facilities offered to trade are not more than equaled at any point in the possession of the United States. The Great ——— surplus of circulation medium has ran articles of merchandise to an enormous height. And so it must remain as long as the mountains continue to give the laborer such liberal rewards for their industry.

Take all circumstances surrounding us as a people we have great cause to be thankful we periled everything but honor to reach this golden land. Our lives and property has been suspended on the most trivial casualty. If but one single mishap had taken place what would have been the result-starvation in the parching lands in the Andes of N.A. But this existence we still have, and it is hardly worth contending for a life in this country not worth appreciating. No quarreling, wrangling or other matters strife. All excitement when you meet your neighbor he asks after some speculation, not after your welfare. To have a social conversation is a great rarity. Politics and religion are lost in the rage of gain. We have a few preachers who preach to empty seats, a congregation paying the jesters regard to them.

One little coincidence I must relate. I attended the house of worship on Lord's Day and at the hour appointed the minister, for so he called himself, raised and made his remarks to just the number there was of the apostles after the transgression of Judas, a forlorn hope for a city congregation where 4000 abided. Thus things and casualties transpired through the first winter in San Francisco, the great commercial depot of California. About the month of February 1849 Mr. H.B. Hoppe who lived at San Jose visited this place, and having made our acquaintance in passing thither he set me to go with him to the Pueble de San Jose. I readily consented so off we started at a full Mexican gate (sic). When we arrived I soon met with my old friends Branhan, Osborns, Wests, Campbell and Cook. I felt very much like I was at home. I purchased a lot 50 feet* square, remained one week, purchased 10,000 feet of lumber and returned to San Francisco. Employed in the meantime a team to come after myself and family in one month's time. The team came according to contract, we all with one accord left San Francisco cheerfully. I made during my stay there, near 3000 dollars. This enabled me to pay for the lot and lumber. We are now in San Jose.

San Jose is beautifully situated in the valley of the same name at the south end of the bay of San Francisco. It (the valley) was settled about the year 1770 by a colony from Castile in old Spain. They have been and are now mixed with the Indian race, but still they maintain their national character as to hospitality and humor. In a general way they are fond of gaming, dancing and being on horseback. Throwing the lariat is a favorite amusement. They do not indulge in drinking ardent spirits to the extent that might be expected compared with Americans. The lower class are given to stealing (the males). The females are very accommodating so much so that a night's lodging can be procured for a trifle with the most of them high or low class. I have before stated that they were Catholics. The Anarchy and misrule of their fiendish rulers has caused them to be more or less jealous of their privileges. A republican form of government is pretended to be given them when in fact it is far far from what they really have.

During the year 1849 the Military Commander, vis: Gov. Riley issued a proclamation convening a convention to form a State Constitution which was done and the first legislature convened under the constitution in December of that year. Many good and wholesome laws, were enacted. The officers of State were made, P.H. Burnett being Governor. All things worked well and apparently to the satisfaction of our rising state. When the admission of California was discussed in Congress to our great dismay she could not be admitted without violating some of the great would-be principals of our confederacy, which has left us in a most deplorable situation.

(Here there seemed to be several pages missing)

As the political horizon appears so darkened at this time I will proceed to give a short discourse on the subject, and as the parties, Democratic and Republican parties, are at antagonistical points it would be necessary to give some of the points of difference between those parties.

As all the great issues grow out of the all absorbing question of slavery that will be the first to some extent discussed. I shall begin with the Fugitive Slave Law.

Running back a little over two centuries we find the Puritan Fathers more just, honest and determined to do justice than their illustrious sons of the present day.
This is the law of 1643:

"It is agreed that if any servant run away from his master into any of those confederate jurisdictions that in such case upon certificate of one Magistrate in the jurisdiction out of which the said servant fled, or upon other due proof, the said servant shall be delivered either to his master or any other —— and brings such certificate of proof" (Winthrop N. Eng. Vol. 2, page 1904-1905).

The Act of congress of 1793 to surrender fugitive from labor came for adjudication before the Supreme Court and it was there decided and affirmed to be constitutional in every State Court in the United States up to the passage of the act of 1850. It was affirmed in the case of Priggs vs —— by the Supreme Court of U.S. to be a constitutional law. I might say that all the courts and all Federal officers from 1793 to 1850 recognized and decided the above quoted laws to be constitutional. We find in Howards Supreme Court Reports, two cases decided together Ableman vs Booth and the U.S. vs Booth, which decision is able and eloquent which commend the reading to all men. Again in the case of the Supreme Court of Wisconsin a right was claimed under the constitution and laws of the U.S. and the decision was against the right claimed and the court of Wis. refused obedience to the writ of error and regarded its own judgment as final and thereby annulling the judgment of the Supreme Court of the U.S. (Howards Report Vol.

20, page 522.)

Various other cases could be brought forward to substantiate the fact that all the decisions of the Supreme Court from 1793 to 1850 where the Fugitive Slave Law was in question decided that it was constitutional and by all the Federal officers and every one that had the execution of the fugitive slave laws, they was carried out and acted upon as constitutional and from 1850 there has something been found out that was not known before. (vis)

That the Fugitive Slave Law was unconstitutional and that Congress had no power under the constitution to pass a Fugitive Slave law, notwithstanding all the officers of Government are sworn to support the constitution of the U.S. and the decisions of the U.S. Court being the interpretation of the constitution. Now in the face of all the decrees, decisions and action of Congress made and provided in such cases they have in 9 states of this confederacy totally failed to notice the said fugitive slave code by passing laws or resolutions so as to prevent the execution of said Slave Code. Now take all this in connection with the fact the the officers are sworn to support the Constitution of the United States.

JAMES C. SIMS

Attorney-at-Law

Clunie Building, 505 California Street

San Francisco, Cal.

Jan. 14, 1903

Mrs. A. H. Sale,

Astoria, Ore:

Dear Aunt Joe:

Enclosed you will please find - the May Family Genealogy - I have followed Grandfather's spelling as well as making a true copy of his record.

The family at this writing are all well — but quite lonesome.

With love to all from all
I remain your loving nephew
Ben

FAMILY RECORD OF RICHARD MARTIN MAY

Commencing as far back as the year A.D. 1709.
This manuscript contains the genealogy of the family up to my Great, Great Grandfather, which was Daniel May from Wales. The following was taken from the Family Record in possession of Henry May of Calloway County, Mo. this February 1856.

R. M. M.

My Grand Mother was of Irish Descent: her maiden name was Loggins.

R. M. M.

(Mother's side) My mother's maiden name was Martin. She had two brothers and three sisters, all of which married Clarksons; one of her brothers now lives in Livingstone Co. Missouri (viz) James Martin.

Daniel May was born in the year of our Lord 1709.
Henry May his oldest son, was born the 22nd of February, 1732 and Gabriel May was born 29th January, 1754 (G.G. Father). Henry May, my father was born 1st January, 1777. My mother Nancy May was born April 6, 1780 and married 5th July, 1798. My Grand Mother May was (a daughter of Sylvannus Stokes) born 22nd April, 1759.
Oney died Nov. 20, 1817. Henry H. died Jan. 21, 1843.

NAMES OF BROTHERS AND SISTERS

Gabriel May	born	3-Aug.	1800
Richard M. May	born	30-Sept.	1802
Priscilla May	born	18-Nov.	1804
Frances May	born	27-Oct.	1806
Oney May	born	17-Dec.	1808
John B. May	born	18-Aug.	1810

Susan May	born	24-Nov.	1812
H. H. May	born	5-Feb.	1817
Matilda E.	born	12-Feb.	1820

DEATHS

Henry	died	3rd-Sept.	1841
William J.	died	19th Sept.	1855
Amanda F.	died	9th Mar.	1842
James Richard	died	4th May	1858

(Born still, 1850 in San Jose, California.)

NAMES AND BIRTHS OF MY CHILDREN

Henry May	Aug. 6th	1831
Angelina May	April 26th	1833
Nancy Martina May	May 16	1835
Josephine May	May 2	1837
William Jennings May	April 5	1839
Elizabeth Matilda May	Jan. 10	1841 }twins
Amanda Franklin May	Jan. 10	1841
James Richard May	Dec. 27	1842
Henriett May	Mar. 1	1845
John Gabriel May	April 23	1848
Stillborn daughter	Mar. 18	1950

RECORD OF R. M. MAY'S FAMILY

Richard Martin May and Robinette Crump was married the 17th, December, 1829.

Henry May father of R.M. May, died the 30th October 1851 in Calloway County, Missouri, at the age of 74 years and 10 months, having lived in the State of Missouri 33 years.

Nancy May consort of the above, died 19th of February, 1861 near 82 years of age having lived 9 years and 4 months a widow, was buried in Family Burrying ground in Calloway County 1 mile below Portland, Missouri. My father H. May was born in Virginia, Pittsylvania County, removed with his Father in 1789 to Kentucky; married 1798; settled on Salt River in Nelson County, Ky. I was born in S. Nelson Co. 1802. Removed to Missouri in 1819 lived in Calloway County 16 years. There married Robinette Crump. who was born 1805 in Clark Co., Ky., on the waters of the Big Slour 8 miles from Winchester where her father, (James Crump) died in 1812. Myself and family left Boone County, Missouri on the 7th of May 1848 arrived in Independence on the 10th and on the 12th left that place for Oregon and for want of company had to pass on to California and reached the town of San Francisco the 11th Nov., 1848. Lived in this place until 20th March, 1849, then removed to San Jose and lived there until 25th. Oct. 1850. Then removed to Oak Grove 1 and ½ miles from San Jose. Lived at this place one year. Removed to Alder Springs Hotel in Sacramento County. Remained there 9 months. On the 12th, Aug., 1852 left Alder Springs for Oregon Territory, arrived in Salem 28th same month. Remained in Salem 1 month then removed to claim called Fir Grove where, R.M. May now lives this 28th day of Sept. 1852, in Marion Co. O. T.

Sold my claim and bought Marion Hotel in Salem and took possession of Hotel the 11th May 1857 and have kept a public house until now 1st. June, 1859. Sold Marion Hotel 2nd Nov. 1859. Remained in Salem.

MARRIAGES OF THE MAY FAMILY

Nancy Martina May married B. F. Rector on the 18th. June, 1857 by Rev. Prarno.

Angelina May and James Rowland Sites was married on the 30th January, 1859 at the same time Josephine May married

Anderson Harris Sale. The above marriage took place at Salem in Marion Hotel O. T. by the Rev. Eider McCarty.

Elizabeth Matilda May married Edward Bolter on the 28th day of July 1861 at the same time and place Henriett May was married to Daniel W. Cox by the Rev. Mr. Rutledge in salem in the State of Oregon. ——Robinette May died this 22nd day of March 1875. Richard Martin May died this 11th day of May 1875.

THE FOLLOWING IS AN ABSTRACT OF MY WIFE'S FAMILY
Her father James Crump was born Jan. 1st, 1776 (descent Welsh). Her mother's maiden name was Betsy Ann Franklin Tucker Ballinger, daughter of Richard and Betsy Ann Ballinger born 18th Nov. 1784, and married 25th Dec. 1801. The Turner connexion is on the Father's side. The Simpson connexion is on the Mother's side.

THE NAMES AND BIRTHS OF MY WIFE'S BROTHERS AND SISTERS.

Estham B. Crump, 10th December, 1802
Henry Simpson and Samuels Renshaw Crump (twins) was born 18th Feb. 1807.
Robinette Crump, 22nd April, 1805
James Alvin Crump 14th June, 1809
Angelina Crump 13th Sept., 1811
HALF BROTHERS AND SISTERS
John B.C. Brown, 31st March, 1817
Mildred B. Brown, 5th June, 1818
Francine L. Brown, 1st July, 1820
L.F.J. Brown, 18th Dec., 1823
Amanda, 15th April, 1826
Mariann Mitchell, 4th April, 1829

My wife's father James Crump died 16th August 1812. Her mother died, 11th May, 1830. John B.C. Brown, half brother died July 31st, 1817.

COLOPHON

The Richard M. May, A SKETCH OF A MIGRATING FAMILY TO CALIFORNIA IN 1848 *was printed in the workshop of Glen Adams, which is located in the quiet country village of Fairfield, southeast Spokane County in Washington state, and one township removed from the Idaho line. The book was keyboarded by Pat Nigh using a Model 7300 Editwriter computer photosetter. It was set in 14 on 16 Janson, a Dutch type face that has stood the test of time. The running heads and page numbers are in 12 point Quill. Photography/darkroom work was by Vern Stevens using a Model 660 DS 24 inch camera and a 25 inch LogE automatic film developing machine. The film was stripped by Vern Stevens who also made the printing plates. The sheets were printed by Vern Stevens using a 28 inch Heidelberg press, model KORS. Folding was by Garry Adams using a three stage Baum Dial-O-Matic folding machine. The books were assembled by Garry Adams. Adhesive paper binding was by Glen Adams and Garry Adams using a Sulby adhesive binding machine. The paper stock is 70 pound Island Offset, a Canadian sheet. This was a fun project. We had no special difficulty with the work. This is the 498th book to come from Ye Galleon Press.*

DATE DUE